the complete guide to the

horse

the complete guide to the

horse

deborah frowen

BARRON'S

Main Photography by Kit Houghton and Sally Anne Thompson

The Complete Guide to the Horse

First edition for the United States and Canada published by Barron's Educational Series, Inc., 1999.

All inquiries should be addressed to:
Barron's Educational Series, Inc.
250 Wireless Boulevard
Hauppauge, NY 11788
http://www.barronseduc.com

Library of Congress Catalog Card No.: 99-63678
International Standard Book No.: 0-7641-5206-8

This is a Prima Editions Book
Text and design © 1999 Prima Editions, England

For Prima Editions
Editorial Director: Roger Kean
Creative Director: Oliver Frey
Series Editor: Iain MacGregor
Copy Editor: Warren Lapworth
Cover Design: Keith Williams
Interior Design: Paul Chubb, Charlotte Kirby
Four-Color Separation: Prima Creative Services, England

Printed and bound in India by Thomson Press

Picture Credits:
COVER Kit Houghton (five images)

AKG: 17, 17; AKG, illustration H.Berghaus (after George Catlin): 14-15; AKG, illustration Elizabeth Butler: 16; AKG, illustration Christian Speyer: 15 top right; AKG, illustration Harold von Schmidt: 13. AKG, illustration Carl Wimar: 12; Animals Unlimited: 74 top left; Bridgeman Art Library, illustration George Stubbs: 30, 32 top, 34; Kit Houghton: 1, 2-3, 6, 7, 18, 19, 19, 20, 21, 22-23, 24-25, 25 top right, 27, 27, 28, 29, 31, 32-33, 33, 35, 36-37, 37 top left, 42 bottom right, 43 bottom, 44 top, 45 top, 46, 50, 54 bottom left, 58 top right, 59 bottom left, 62 bottom right, 76 bottom, 77, 84 top right, 89 top right, 94-95, 95 top right, 98, 98, 98, 98, 99, 99, 99, 99, 99, 99, 99, 99, 99, 100-101, 101, 102, 103, 104, 105, 106, 107, 110, 111, 112, 113, 114-115, 116, 117, 118-119, 120-121, 120, 121, 122, 122, 123, 124-125, 125, 126, 127, 128, 128, 129, 130, 131, 132, 132-133, 134, 135, 136, 136-137, 137, 138, 139, 141 top left, 142, 143, 144, 145, 145, 145, 145, 145, 145, 145, 145, 146, 146, 146, 146, 147, 147, 148, 148, 148, 148, 149, 150, 150, 151, 151, 152, 153, 153, 153, 153, 153, 153, 154, 154, 154, 154, 154, 155, 155, 156, 156, 156-157, 157, 157, 158-159, 164, 165, 165, 166-167, 167, 168, 168, 169, 169, 170, 171, 171, 172, 173, 174-175, 175, 175, 176-177, 177, 178-179, 180, 181, 182, 182-183, 184-185, 185, 189; Bob Langrish: 9 bottom right, 10-11, 77 top right, 78 top, 84 bottom, 88 top left, 89 bottom right, 90 top left, 91 bottom right; Sally Anne Thompson: 8-9, 23 top left, 26, 38, 38, 39, 39, 40, 41, 41, 42 top left, 43 top right, 44 bottom left, 45 bottom right, 47, 47, 48, 48, 49, 51, 51, 53 bottom, 54 top, 55, 55, 56, 57, 58 bottom, 59 top right, 60, 60, 61, 61, 62 top left, 63, 63, 64, 64, 65, 65, 66, 66, 67, 67, 68, 68, 69, 69, 70, 71, 71, 72, 72, 73, 73, 74-75, 76 top left, 78 bottom right, 79, 80, 80, 81 bottom right, 82, 82, 83, 83, 85, 85, 86, 86, 87 top left, 88 top right, 88 bottom left, 90 top right, 91 top left, 91 top right, 92, 92, 93, 93, 96, 97, 97, 98, 99, 99, 108, 140-141; R. Willbie: 52, 52, 53 top, 81 top, 87 bottom.

9 8 7 6 5 4 3 2

introduction

As we enter the twenty-first century and inhabit a world increasingly dependent on technological advances, it is easy to consider the horse only in terms of recreation and sport. Millions enjoy riding as a pastime and even more enjoy watching the sporting horse in action; but few people today can remember the horse at work. Yet for thousands of years the horse fulfilled an essential role in everyday life.

Until the development of the railroad, and later the automobile, the horse was the mainstay of land-based

transport and communications. The predominance of horse-drawn farm equipment until the mid-nineteenth century also characterized the face of farming. Horses remained an integral part of agricultural life until mechanization tightened its grip.

Since its domestication some 5,000 years ago, the story of the horse has been inextricably linked with the progress of mankind in times of war, as well as peace. The mobility it conferred upon man expanded horizons that in turn led to the creation, and destruction, of great empires. While the increasing sophistication of weaponry meant that the horse's role in war changed through the ages, they played their part

well into the twentieth century; they were employed in large numbers in both World Wars.

This book aims to show the horse in all of its roles, past and present. In addition to a section on the sports and recreational pastimes with which the horse is associated, a major part of the book is dedicated to the influence and development of the world's breeds, including more than 120 types of horse and pony.

Owning a horse is a full-time responsibility, but a healthy and contented animal must be the ultimate aim of anyone whose life is connected with this most noble of creatures. The final section of the book therefore looks at the physiology, behavior, and management of the horse.

The horse remains a complex creature, so establishing any kind of lasting relationship takes time. But as anyone who has had any contact with horses will know, it is an effort well worth making. Once a bond has been forged you will be rewarded by the horse's unquestioning loyalty and trust.

This book aims to increase knowledge and understanding and thus ensure that any relationship between horse and human is enhanced.

development of the
horse

The development of the modern horse became much clearer in the mid-nineteenth century, with the discovery in America of a skeleton of a small animal named *Eohippus* by scientists.

left: *Man has always been in awe of the grace, speed, and power of the horse, and prehistoric cave paintings capture these glorious attributes in a manner as lively as the real animals galloping through water.*

the **pre-domestic** horse

The history of the modern horse became much clearer in the mid-nineteenth century, with the discovery in the United States of a skeleton of a small animal named *Eohippus* by scientists. It is from this small creature, similar in size to a fox, that the modern horse has evolved. *Eohippus*, or the dawn horse, as it is also referred to, developed from a group of animals

known as Condylarths, which inhabited the earth about 75 million years ago and from which all hoofed creatures are believed to have descended.

Subsequent reconstructions of remains show that *Eohippus* probably stood between 10 and 14 inches (25–35.5 cm) high at the shoulder, had a hunched back and short legs with splayed toes—four on the fore feet,

three on the hind feet. The toes were padded to enable it to move across soft, marshy land; and these pads are present on the modern horse as ergots—horny growths on the back of the fetlocks.

The dawn horse was eventually succeeded by *mesohippus, miohippus,* then *merychippus.* Each type was larger than the last, with a gradual change

Migrations of these early examples of horses took place across land bridges that connected Asia with North America and Europe with Africa until the end of the Ice Age. There is still no explanation for the horse becoming extinct in the American continents around 8,000 years ago. Horses were not re-introduced to the Americas until the sixteenth century.

Equus developed into four primitive types that evolved according to their environment. In Asia it became the steppe horse (*Equus caballus przewalskii poliakov*, or the Asian Wild Horse, the only surviving member of this primitive group); in eastern Europe the light-limbed plateau horse known as the Tarpan (*Equus przewalskii gmelini antonius*); in northern Europe the heavier, slower Forest Horse (*Equus przewalskii silvaticus*); and in northeast Siberia the Tundra, from which Yakut ponies, native to this area, are believed to have descended.

Further studies into early equine structure made during the twentieth century revealed the likelihood of four further subspecies of *Equus* that existed prior to its domestication some 5–6,000 years ago. Horse type 1 was similar in type to the British Exmoor Pony. This small, sturdy animal inhabited the area of northwest Europe and was able to withstand harsh conditions. Horse type 2 was a coarser, heavier type of horse that roamed the lands of northern Eurasia and resembled the Asian Wild Horse. Its modern-day equivalent is the Highland pony. Horse type 3 was a lean, narrow, thin-skinned animal from Central Asia capable of surviving in harsh desert conditions. Its characteristics are similar to those of the Akhal-Teké. Horse type 4 was a finely built, heat-resistant desert horse from Western Asia that closely resembled the Caspian Pony.

of features, such as the back becoming straighter and the limbs longer. The feet still had three toes, but the central one was the largest and bore the most weight.

As the earth's environment changed—jungle giving way to plains and steppes, where vegetation comprised low-lying grasses—the horse continued to adapt, gradually evolving into the shape we recognize today. The neck became longer, allowing the horse to reach down to graze, and the teeth developed to accommodate this pattern of eating.

As its natural hiding places were lost, the horse developed capabilities that allowed it to survive. Its legs became more elongated, with powerful muscles at the tops of the legs to facilitate speed, and the skull became larger, with eye sockets farther to the side to enable all-around vision.

evolution of Equus

The first single-hoofed horse, *pliohippus*, evolved some six million years ago as a prototype of the first true horse, *Equus caballus*, which emerged some five million years later.

the horse through the ages

Ever since it was first domesticated, the horse has been an integral part of man's life, giving him the power to conquer and rule. With the industrial revolution of the eighteenth century and the subsequent growth of urban populations, the horse continued to rule the road, pulling everything from trains to funeral wagons. Even in death the horse proved its worth, every part of its body being utilized. While in the modern world the horse is largely used for leisure, it is still inextricably linked to many parts of our life and traditions.

the Plains Indians

Spanish conquerors reintroduced the horse into the Americas during the sixteenth century and in so doing brought about the horse culture of the Plains Indians—the last of the world's great "horse people."

For the American Indians, the horse not only provided a way of hunting buffalo effectively, but also provided an essential form of transport, allowing them to move camp more easily. In the tribal world, the horse was a symbol of

below: *Indian ponies were tough, enduring, and very fast. They were ideal for the types of terrain and enemies the Native Americans had to contend with.*

left: *The reintroduction of the horse to the Americas in the sixteenth century brought about the horse culture of the Plains Indians.*

wealth and nobility—a powerful Indian often owned as many as 40 horses at any one time—as well as a near-necessity of life. Without it, hunting buffalo was almost impossible, and buffalo provided food, clothing, and the means to construct shelters—commodities similar to those the horse provided for early man.

While Indian ponies were often coarse and uninspiring to look at, they were undoubtedly tough, enduring, and very fast. Once the Indians had acquired horses, they began to breed from them, most notably the Nez Percé Indians, who developed the Appaloosa horse by initiating a strict selective breeding policy. A similar culture was developing at the same time in South America, from which the modern-day Indian cowboys (gauchos) descend.

The Indian horse culture lasted for about 200 years, until the 1870s, when the United States government implemented policies that ensured its demise. While the horse undoubtedly changed the course of history for the Plains Indians and enriched American history, the Indian horse culture left no lasting legacy.

the American cowboy

Not only did the Spanish bring the horse to the New World, they also brought the tradition of ranching. However, it was not until the nineteenth century, when cattle were in great demand for their meat rather

than their skin, that the huge commercial ranches of western America sprang up and brought with them the need for vast numbers of cattle horses. Initially, wild Mustangs were brought in as mounts for the American cowboys, but later on other breeds, such as the Quarter Horse—considered the finest "cow" pony in the world, due to its speed, balance, and agility—were also used. Such qualities were essential for a horse that was required, among other things, to

above: *On the attack: the Indian at war. The horse brought more mobility for foraging further afield, and making war on neighbors and invaders alike.*

"cut" or separate a specific steer from a herd, or keep a taut line between itself and its quarry, even after its rider had dismounted.

With the rise of the American cowboy came the need for suitable saddlery and clothing. Although variations existed in different parts of the country, the Western saddle was based on the saddle brought over by the Spanish; it continued to evolve as ranching techniques advanced. The saddle was designed for comfort and practicality. Lassos were attached to the prominent horn at the front, and the wide, roomy stirrups were constructed from wood and leather for warmth.

Clothing worn then is still used today in traditional Western riding, including the broad-brimmed hat, known as the Stetson after its maker, John B. Stetson (1830–1906), which not only protects the rider from the elements but doubles as a drinking vessel.

left: *The horse gave the Indians the necessary speed to hunt buffalo effectively. Thus, they were able to sustain themselves over the coming winter months.*

the horse at war

From the dawn of the world's earliest civilizations to the first part of the twentieth century, the horse played a valuable role in warfare. Initially it was confined to transporting the soldier to and from the battlefield. In this role alone it changed the course of history, by mobilizing armies and giving them the power to create, and destroy, huge empires.

The invention of the saddle and stirrups heralded a new era for the war horse. Once so attired, the horse provided a secure base from which the soldier could launch attacks, and thus effective tactical warfare began. Skillful horse warriors, the twelfth-century Mongols were able to conquer the largest land-mass empire ever known. The Hungarian Hussars adopted a

bent-knee, short-stirrup seat that provided an effective position from which to attack.

The use of heavy protective armor, which was vital as the striking power of weaponry increased, led to the development of the great war horses of the Middle Ages, which were expected to carry as much as 480 pounds (222.6 kg) in weight. The invention of

gunpowder and the subsequent need for a horse more suited to reconnaissance, raiding, and pursuit led to the develpment of a smaller, more agile type of battle horse.

Modern-day competition breeds such as the Hannoverian and Trakehner were originally bred as troop horses, while the Waler, or Australian Stock Horse as it is now known, was frequently used as a remount by the British Army. By the late nineteenth century the Thoroughbred was seen as the most suitable mount for a British officer. In the United States, the tough and versatile Morgan Horse was favored by the army.

Immortalized in great paintings of the nineteenth century, the horse can be seen at its valiant best charging into battle, but sadly the outcome was often tragic. In the campaign involving the Charge of the Light Brigade at Balaclava during the Crimean War (1854–1856), the cavalry lost the majority of its 2,000 horses.

Modern warfare requires the horse to play a less significant role than it once did, but still millions were employed during both World Wars. Its role was largely confined to transportation—especially on the European battlefields, where horses were expected to carry as much as 300 pounds (136 kg) of ammunition, feed, and additional equipment. The cavalry continued to exert its power farther afield, however, most notably during the 1917–1918 Palestine Campaign, where about 20,000 cavalrymen, led by General Sir Edmund Allenby, fought back the Turks.

While a majority of armies accepted the inevitable move toward mechanization, some countries, notably Germany, Russia, and Poland, continued to rely on horses for transport, and to a lesser extent cavalry, during the Second World War. Military horses are now largely confined to ceremonial duties, but there are some places in the world where the horse is still relied on in conflict. In the 1980s, for example, the Mujahideen took to the saddle to fight off the Russians in Afghanistan.

the working horse

Until the early twentieth century, the horse played an essential role in industry and transport. Before railroads and automobiles, the horse was the only effective means of transport. Even after the development of railroads, horses were employed by the thousands to move raw material and goods to and from trains. Commercial breeding of heavy horses continued due to their usefulness in and around freight yards.

As a result of the industrial revolution and the spread of railroads, coal became a vital commodity; horses and ponies were used in the mining industry well into the twentieth century. Horse power was essential for canal transport, particularly in Britain, whose system of waterways was arguably the most comprehensive in the world. Canal barges were pulled by "boaters," normally light draft horses no bigger than 15.2 hands (62.2 ins; 158 cm) that could pass underneath the tow bridges.

Horses were utilized in great numbers in the fledgling lumber industry in the United States and Canada. Initially, mules and lighter draft animals were used, until heavier European breeds were introduced during the nineteenth century. Horses are still used by foresters in many countries.

transport

The horse was an integral part of almost every aspect of nineteenth-century life. Until the introduction of the electric trolley and the automobile, the horse was the exclusive means of public transport. The first regular bus service was run in Paris in 1828, followed a year later by a similar one in Britain. By 1869 there were more than 2,000 buses operating in London alone.

Horses were employed in firefighting, in funeral processions, in breweries, to deliver food, and as taxicabs. But in the nineteenth century a total reliance on the horse brought a problem— pollution caused by manure.

left: *Once emmigration was underway in the eighteenth and nineteenth centuries to the New World and the British Commonwealth, man's use of the horse was fundamental in the construction of the new states.*

In many parts of the world farming is now totally reliant on machinery, but there are some countries, especially in eastern Europe, where the horse remains an integral part of agricultural life.

a modern role

While it is no longer as integral to our life as in previous centuries, the horse still plays its part. Most countries in the world have a token cavalry unit, as well as a more significant mounted police force. The most famous example is probably the Mounties (The Royal Canadian Mounted Police Force), although many countries including the United States, England, Australia, India, Italy, and Spain, have mounted forces. Mounted police first appeared in the eighteenth century in London, where they were used to keep public order, a function they still fulfill today.

The horse remains a symbol of pomp and ceremony throughout the world, but nowhere is this pageantry more apparent than in England, where the monarchy continues to use horses and elaborate coaches for all state occasions.

communication and agriculture

Horses have always played a part in communication. Mail coaches were in service in Europe and North America by the late 1700s, but earlier postal systems, using mounted postboys and mail carts, had been around since the beginning of the century. The American Pony Express service (1860–1862) used relays of riders to carry mail along the 1,966-mile (3,164-km) route between Missouri and Sacramento. By the end of the nineteenth century, a more sophisticated postal system used railroads, although horses were still needed for deliveries from the stations.

For thousands of years—until the eighteenth century—the principal use of the horse was for warfare. Horses were too precious to work the land, so this role was filled by oxen, which were still used in many cultures long after the farm horse was in use elsewhere.

The system of crop rotation farming, introduced in the eighteenth century, led to the invention of increasingly sophisticated equipment and in turn the development of the heavy horse, which was better suited to working with it than oxen. Horse-drawn machines invented during this period revolutionized farming; the most famous were probably the seed drill, designed by Jethro Tull, and the swing plow. In North America, huge numbers of horses worked the vast acreage—by the 1940s, when mechanization had once more transformed the face of farming, about 20 million horses were out of work.

classical equitation

Classical riding at its highest level is known as *haute école* or high school, and has its roots in Ancient Greece. Xenophon, a cavalry officer and historian, was the author of two books, *Hippike* and *Hipparchikos*, which contained advice and described techniques that continue to influence modern classical equitation.

In the Middle Ages, the horse was used mostly by noblemen, as a vehicle for war. This was the age of jousting and chivalry. Command of his charger required precision, so the soldier turned to severe methods, with aggressive bits and spurs substituting for training.

Free time for the aristocrats of Europe brought benefits for the horse in the form of more sophisticated thinking that had its roots in the work of Xenophon. Notable trainers experimenting with classical theories by the mid-sixteenth century were Count Cesare Fiaschi and his pupil Federico Grisone. Their methods used implements such as hot irons to encourage horses to go forward. It was not until Grisone's pupil Giovanni Baptista Pignatelli began working that a more recognizably modern system evolved.

Pignatelli was responsible for devising movements that required lengthy training, rather than force. Gradually his work became known throughout Europe as his students became teachers themselves. One of these, Antoine de Pluvinel, trainer to King Louis XIII of France, followed Pignatelli in refusing to apply cruel methods. Men such as de Pluvinel were to have a profound influence on the figure regarded as the founding father of classical equitation, François Robichon de la Guerinière.

De la Guerinière, who was born in 1688, generally used English Thoroughbreds at his riding school at the Tuileries in Paris. He trained the men who were to develop his style and philosophy at the two centers that today are still the greatest ambassadors for classical training—the Spanish Riding School in Vienna and the Cadre Noir, at Saumur in France. Both schools demonstrate the highest levels of achievement in classical riding. Audiences around the world have been treated to displays of famous movements likened to ballet with horses.

left: *Founded in 1560, the Spanish Riding School in Vienna is one of the most celebrated equestrian institutes in the world.*

right: *Serious training is required for a horse to be able to perform the precise movements of haute école.*

the Spanish Riding School

The Spanish Riding School of Vienna was founded in 1560 and at the time was one of many such establishments where intensive training of horse and rider was undertaken. The school derives its name from the Spanish blood of its horses, the gray Lipizzaners that were bred at the Imperial stables in Vienna beginning in the sixteenth century.

Young horses at the Spanish school start their serious education at the age of three, when they begin working on the lunge. This is the beginning of a long process that builds the muscular framework required to carry out the precise movements of *haute école*, such as half-passes, pirouettes, and flying changes.

The history of the Spanish Riding School is full of setbacks, its survival linked closely with the Austro-Hungarian emperors. In 1918,

left: *Lipizzaners have been used at the Spanish Riding School since the sixteenth century.*

movements, such as shoulder-in, half-pirouette, and rein-back. Pupils are also encouraged to gain an all-around education, to improve techniques for cross-country and show-jumping.

haute école

Haute école is divided into airs on and above the ground. The piaffe and passage performed by Olympic dressage riders are airs on the ground. The Lipizzaners of the Spanish school are taught to perform piaffe in-hand. Tours by the Cadre Noir are as popular as those of their counterparts in Vienna, with displays including the so-called Black Mass, performed by the instructors or *ecuyers*. The Black Mass covers walk, trot, canter, and passage, while the second display by the *sauteurs* consists of airs above the ground.

Airs above the ground include the levade, the courbette, the ballotade, and the capriole, which are all performed in-hand or under saddle. The movements are devised to reflect the kind of activity seen in young horses at play in their natural untrained state.

In the levade, the hind legs are moved under the body, thus taking the weight off the forehand and lifting the forelegs off the ground. To be performed correctly, the hocks are bent at a 45-degree angle and the horse literally squats on his haunches. It is in moving forward from this position with a jump into the air that the courbette is performed. When all four feet leave the ground, instead of assuming the position of the levade, the body is horizontal, and the hind legs are pulled under the horse, this is the ballotade. The final movement consists of stretching the hind legs behind the body to perform the capriole.

following the end of the First World War and the collapse of the Austro-Hungarian Empire, the school was threatened with closure when it was taken over by the state. Chief rider Moritz Herold is regarded as its savior. He started a fundraising campaign and had the vision to see the future of the school in public performances. In July 1920 the school gave its first such performance and embarked on the road to bringing classical equitation to a far wider audience than de la Guerinière could ever have imagined.

the Cadre Noir

The Spanish school's influence spread to the cavalry school of the Cadre Noir at Saumur, France, through

left: *The levade is one of the airs above the ground. The other movements are the courbette, ballotade, and capriole.*

civilian instructors who traveled from Vienna to work alongside military trainers. The French academy arrived at its present home in 1814.

Disputes between the Spanish school's civilian trainers and their military counterparts caused a rift and the school was closed for three years, between 1822 and 1825. When it reopened, the military wing had gained the upper hand, and it dominated until the 1960s.

Today, teaching at the school combines both approaches, with classical equitation as taught at both Versailles and Vienna blending with the military establishment's focus on training for cross-country riding. To attend the school, pupils have to be recommended as ready for this high level of instruction. Training is given to improve the seat and balance, concentrating on working without stirrups. Dressage exercises to improve the airs include work on lateral

breeds of the
world

above: *The Exmoor Pony is one of Britain's oldest native breeds.*

left: *American Standardbreds can be traced back to the English Thoroughbred.*

A comprehensive guide to the wide variety of horse and pony breeds that span the globe details their history, characteristics, and physical features, and serves as a valuable reference to the buyer and equine lover alike.

influence of the Arabian

The Arabian, with its flamboyant nature and proud bearing, is one of the most distinctive breeds of horse, and since the Second World War it has become one of the most popular. Renowned for its beauty, grace, and fiery temperament, the Arabian breed has been most commonly associated with the show ring, but in the latter half of the century has been increasingly appreciated for its speed, endurance, and all-around athleticism.

While there are disputes surrounding its early history, the Arab is recorded as the earliest purebred, found across the Middle East, originally as a war horse but also historically for sport, chariot racing, and an early form of polo. Agile and light-boned, the breed evolved as a desert horse, able to withstand extremes of heat and cold and the paucity of grazing.

One of the earliest exporters of the breed from its native Arabia was

Wilfrid Blunt who, with his wife Lady Anne, established the world-famous Crabbet Stud in England. Through her three Crabbet-born fillies, foundation mare Rodania was the beginning of probably the most

left: *The Arab has a distinctive appearance with its dished face, wide forehead tapering to a neat muzzle, and large, low-set eyes.*

important line of purebreds. Equally influential were the stallions Mahruss II and Messoud, who came from Ali Pasha Sherif's stud in Egypt. In the Blunts' hands the potential versatility of the breed was already visible. The stallion Kars, a bay warhorse, was not only raced over hurdles within three months of arriving in Britain, but was also hunted and described as a superb jumper.

The first Arab-only race meeting was held at Newmarket, England, in 1884 at the instigation of Wilfrid Blunt. The race included two horses brought to Britain for the occasion from India. However, the outcome was seen as disappointing, in comparison to the well-established Thoroughbred racing.

The contribution of Arab blood to the Thoroughbred is well recorded, with three Arabian sires said to be the founders of the breed: the Byerley Turk, Darley Arabian, and Godolphin Arabian. The first to come to England was the Byerley Turk, who stood at Goldsborough Hall Stud in the late seventeenth century.

types of Arab

Over the centuries, several different types of Arab have evolved. The English Arabs descend mainly from the Egyptian-bred stock imported to Crabbet Stud. Egyptian lines owe much to the stallion Nazeer, whose progeny sired quality offspring through Ibn Halima and Morafic in the United States, and Aswan, who stood at Russia's Tersk Stud.

above: *The Arabian has played a significant part in the development of almost all the world's breeds.*

The Russian Arab, with its athleticism and strong action, has in turn been influential in western breeding, as has the internationally renowned Polish Arab, which arrived in Poland with the Crusaders of the sixteenth century. Polish Arabs are notable for their combination of looks and strength, exemplified by the stallion Piechur, a winner of the Polish Derby, who also had success in the show ring.

The American Arab owes much to the combination of English, Egyptian, and Polish Arab blood. The French Anglo-Arab is one of France's most celebrated riding horse breeds, but in France the emphasis on purebreds is toward the race track, with the resulting creation of a slightly larger, less showy animal.

left: *The Arab is renowned for its beauty, powers of endurance, and all-around athleticism.*

A modern development is the revival of interest in the breed's original homeland, with the return of the most favored bloodlines to the Gulf States. Sheikhs who have enjoyed a passion for Thoroughbred racing over the past three decades are now importing some of the world's best Arab stallions.

Today, the Arab horse is bred in nearly every country in the world and the struggle continues to maintain the true type. Controversy surrounds preoccupation with the show ring and the fashion for an exaggerated action, with the presentation of often hyped-up animals before judges whose attention is focused on a posed showing style, according to critics. The result is that the winners are often not those that would make the best riding horses or ensure long-term survival of the breed's attributes.

the two basic Arab shapes

Broadly, the elegant and graceful Arab can be divided into two types: the larger and slightly coarser-framed racing Arab, and the slighter, more delicate riding and show horse. The Arab has a distinctive broad head with a dished face. The forehead is wide, tapering to a small, neat muzzle, with large nostrils ready to flare at any moment. Large, intelligent eyes are set low beneath small, curved ears.

The breed's capacity as an endurance horse is indicated by a good depth through the heart, a broad, well-developed chest with a laid-back shoulder, and well-sprung ribs. The back is short and level, the thighs strong and well-muscled. Arab legs have short, strong cannon bones, with well-defined tendons. The feet are hard and neat.

Toughness and strength have made the Arab the world's foremost endurance horse. Treadmill tests have highlighted a heart function, blood characteristics, and muscle structure that make the breed superior to others in its ability to cover long distances efficiently. Arabs are bred for speed in many countries where Arab racing is increasingly popular.

To balance its characteristic sensitive nature with modern life, the Arab horse benefits from management that's as natural as possible. Detractors complain that the breed is temperamental, pinpointing a lack of steadiness, while supporters point to the subtleties of this intelligent, highly strung animal that, once understood, are very rewarding. The best are gentle and benefit most from a one-to-one relationship with their handler, which again contributes to the success of the breed as an endurance horse.

The young stock is slow to mature, and most steady work with Arab horses doesn't begin until the age of four. This is the minimum age for Arab-racing in Britain. Likewise, training for and introduction to the sport of endurance doesn't begin until the horse is around six or seven, with success in the sport being achieved well into the teens.

In the show ring, Arabs can be shown either in-hand or ridden. One of the most successful stallions to carry the honors in both spheres in Britain was Sainfoin, winner of the Arab Horse Society's stallion championship on seven occasions in the 1920s and 1930s, a feat unlikely to be seen in modern show rings, where many exhibitors choose to show in-hand or under saddle but not both.

versatility breeds success

Ridden Arab classes are gaining in popularity, pointing to a general acceptance of the benefits of showing the breed to its full potential. Of the success stories at the British Arab Horse Society's national show in this sphere in recent years, the majority of supreme championship ridden winners have been purebreds, with many mares emerging as winners over the stallions.

Supporters of the breed point to its versatility, which dates back to its origins as both a war- and sport horse. Arabs and their crosses were a common sight at the Hurlingham Polo Club in England in

the early days of the development of the sport, with the original polo ponies generally around 13.3 hands high. Gradually, however, the Arab lost out to Thoroughbred crosses as the demands and popularity of the sport grew.

On another playing field entirely, Arab horses are sought after in the sport of carriage driving, especially in the United States, where their sheer presence and quick-wittedness make them stars in the dressage section. The Arab has been no stranger to prizes in the mainstream sport of dressage. One of the early successful combinations to bring the sport to Britain was Henry Wynmalen, whose demonstrations with the gray Shagya Arab stallion Basa earned acclaim nationwide. While today the sport is dominated by Warmbloods, the contribution of Arab blood to the equally charismatic Lipizzaner,

celebrated for its movement and shown off the world over by the Spanish Riding School of Vienna, is clear to see.

To those who dispute the Arab's abilities as a jumper, the success of the breed both in show-jumping and eventing is a surprise. The part-bred Pasha, who partnered Richard Walker to success at Badminton in 1967, was perhaps the most successful in silencing the critics. One of the most outstanding event horses in recent years was Spinning Rhombus, the ride of New Zealander Andrew Nicholson. The horse, whose dam was by the Arab stallion Tammany, was on the New Zealand gold medal-winning team at Stockholm in 1990.

left: *An Arab stallion. The Arab has a distinctive broad head, neat muzzle, large nostrils, and large eyes. Its toughness and strength are legendary, as is its speed.*

development of the Thoroughbred

When racing became fashionable as a result of King Charles II's passion for riding in competition with his courtiers at Newmarket, speed rather than strength became the quality most prized in horses bred for sport. Consequently Englishmen acquired light-framed stallions from the Middle East and Barbs from the Barbary Coast (now Tunisia) to impart speed into the offspring of the more cumbersome native mares whose ancestors bred mounts for men in armor.

Between 1670 and 1740, 103 horses of Eastern blood were imported, but only three—the Byerley Turk, who arrived in about 1687, the Darley Arabian, brought from Aleppo, Syria, in 1704, and the Godolphin Arabian, who began stud duties around 1729—founded male lines that have endured.

The leading breeder in the middle of the eighteenth century was William, Duke of Cumberland, whose stallions included Herod and Eclipse, whose great grandsire was the Darley Arabian. Eclipse was not once extended, let alone beaten, in 18 races, and today about 90 percent of Thoroughbreds in the world descend from him in the male line.

Among the significant sons of Herod was Florizel, the sire of Diomed, who won the first running of the Derby in 1780. Diomed was a disappointment at stud in England, but when sent to the United States, at the age of 21 in 1798 he founded an important male line through his son, Sir Archie. Timoleon, by Sir Archie, sired the foul-tempered Boston, winner of 40 of his 45 races and champion sire in 1851, 1852, and 1853. Among the sons of Boston was Lexington, one of America's greatest stallions. Having won the Great State Post Stakes at New Orleans in 1854 and other races, Lexington retired to stud and was champion sire 16 times.

below: *From the many breeds that were imported during the 1700s, the Arabian from Syria was one of only three that established successful breed lines.*

left: *This oil painting, "Chestnut Mare and Foal" c.1761–1763 by George Stubbs (1724–1806), perfectly illustrates the elegance and grace that breeders were trying to perfect in the 1700s.*

above: *"Mares and Foals" by George Stubbs, c.1762. The Duke of Cumberland was one of the first successful breeders of racehorses in the 1700s.*

below: *Racehorses on the gallops at Newmarket, England. Charles II's love of racing established the desire for speed in horses for this sport.*

Among the most influential of mares at this time was Web, owned by the Fifth Earl of Jersey. Every one of his ten Classic winners descended from her, including the Derby winners Middleton and Bay Middleton, as well as Glencoe, who won the 2000 Guineas in 1834. On being imported to the United States, Glencoe achieved enormous success as his daughters proved a wonderful outcross for Lexington. Lexington's three greatest sons, Kentucky, Asteroid, and Norfolk, were all products of Glencoe mares.

Among the offspring Glencoe left in England was Pocahontas, a broodmare of incomparable consequence as dam of the sires Stockwell, King Tom, and Rataplan. The former seven-times leading sire produced the Derby winners Doncaster—by whom the most important male line of the Darley Arabian and Eclipse was perpetuated—Blair Athol, and Lord Lyon.

success of the dukes' breeding programs

Although horses no longer ran in four-mile heats by the middle of the nineteenth century, stamina was still

right: *The Hackney Horse has both Thoroughbred and Arab blood in its veins, and was much sought after for both military and civilian uses in the 1800s.*

highly esteemed. The ideal horse could demonstrate his versatility by completing the Triple Crown as a three-year-old, before proving his stamina by winning over the two-and-a-half miles of the Gold Cup.

The Sixth Duke of Portland's unbeaten St. Simon was not qualified for the Classics in 1884, but proved his excellence by winning the Gold Cup by 20 lengths, while Isinglass, owned and bred by Colonel Harry McCalmont, won the Triple Crown in 1893 but missed the Gold Cup because of a performance setback. He was kept in training as a five-year-old so that he could put the seal on his career by winning the cup on his only appearance of 1895.

During the late nineteenth century the First Duke of Westminster became

the only man to have bred and owned two Triple Crown winners—Ormonde in 1886 and Flying Fox in 1899. He also bred Sceptre, by Persimmon out of a full sister to Ormonde. Sold as yearling for a then record 10,000 guineas after the duke's death, she won the 2000 Guineas, 1000 Guineas, Oaks, and St. Leger in 1902 before maintaining one of the most important female families in *The General Stud Book*.

In 1904 Pretty Polly emerged as the second great filly of the outset of the twentieth century by winning the 1000 Guineas, Oaks, and St. Leger. Bred by Major Estace Loder of the Eyrefield Lodge Stud on the Curragh, Ireland, Pretty Polly founded a flourishing female line that has produced the Derby winners St. Paddy and Psidium.

An important English breeder of the first half of the twentieth century was the Seventeenth Earl of Derby. Many of his horses were either the offspring or descendants of Gondolette, whom he bought for 1,550 guineas in 1912.

They included her son Sansovino, winner of the Derby in 1924, and Hyperion, winner of the Derby and St. Leger in 1933. Other stallions of note owned by Lord Derby, ten times leading breeder between 1919 and 1945, included the two brothers Fairway and Pharos, the latter of whose son, Nearco, has had incalculable influence on British stock.

Nearco was bred in Italy in 1935 by Federico Tessio and was unbeaten in 14 races, including the Italian Derby by a distance. He was brought to England by the bookmaker Martin Benson, who paid £60,000 for him. Among Nearco's offspring were the Derby winners Dante and Nimbus and the St. Leger winner Sayajirao. Although Nearco was only leading sire twice, he established a dominant male line. Of the 32 winners of the Derby between 1967 and 1998, 22 could be traced to Nearco on their sire's side, nine of them through Northern Dancer. Moreover, Sadler's Wells, a son of Northern Dancer, was leading sire in Britain in eight of the nine seasons between 1990 and 1998.

The influence of Nearco in the United States has been largely due to his sons Nasrullah and Royal Charger, close relatives tracing to Mumtaz Mahal in the female line, as well as of the export to Canada, in utero, of Nearctic, sire of Northern Dancer, who won the Kentucky Derby and the Preakness Stakes in 1964. Lady Angela, paternal grandam of Northern Dancer, comes from the Pretty Polly female line.

In contrast to 100 years ago, when stamina was held in such high esteem, middle-distance excellence is the quality most prized in Britain today, as it has long been the case in the United States. The Kentucky Derby was reduced from a mile-and-a-half to a mile-and-a-quarter in 1895, and the Preakness Stakes from a mile-and-a-half to a mile and one-and-a-half furlongs, in 1888.

The demand made on British breeders is to a large extent reflected by the fact that only two of the 25 Group One races are beyond a mile-and-a-half—the Gold Cup at two-and-a-half miles and the St. Leger at a mile and six furlongs—and that the average distance of the 20 Group One races for three-year-olds or upward is just under a mile-and-a-quarter.

The competition horse

Most of the world's horse breeds have benefited, at some time or other, from the addition of Thoroughbred blood to lend refinement and speed. However, it is in the breeding of competition horses that the Thoroughbred has had the most recent impact.

The growth of the competitive disciplines of show-jumping, three-day eventing, and dressage and carriage driving has led to a demand for elegant but tough and athletic breeds. The German stable of competition horses, which includes the Hanoverian, Holstein, Oldenburg, and Trakehner, have all been influenced by the Thoroughbred to some degree. The latter is probably the closest in appearance to the Thoroughbred, which was used to upgrade the breed as far back as the beginning of the eighteenth century, and it was these two breeds that contributed to the development of the modern-day Hanoverian, probably the most successful of all the German warmbloods. Another renowned international performer, the Selle Français, was developed using imported English Thoroughbreds to cross with their less refined native mares.

The Thoroughbred has also played an influential part in the world of harness racing, where the sport's most important breeds, namely the American Standardbred and the French and Orlov Trotters, all have Thoroughbred roots. The foundation sire of the Standardbred, Messenger, traces back to the Darley Arabian, while the half-bred Young Rattler had the greatest influence on the French breed. In Britain the Hackney Pony and Horse, renowned for its trotting ability in the show ring rather than on the racetrack, has its roots in Shales, a grandson of the first famous racehorse, Flying Childers.

below: *In American harness racing, the American Standardbred and the French and Orlov Trotters all have breed lines stretching back to the Thoroughbred.*

principal horse
breeds

From Akhal-Teké to Wielkopolski, the diversity of the world's horse population has as much to do with man's intervention as with the environment. The following pages detail all the major breeds. Because there is so much cross-breeding involved, cross-referenced page numbers are shown in brackets where appropriate.

Akhal-Teké

height *15.2 h.h. (62.2 ins; 158 cm)*
color *"metallic" chestnut*
conformation *straight profile; thin skin; long, thin neck, set high; narrow body; shallow ribcage; narrow quarters; long, slender legs; small, neat feet*

The Akhal-Teké, bred in the Karakum Desert of Turkmenistan, has probably been in existence for more than 3,000 years. It is the modern equivalent of the Ancient Horse Type 3—the thin-skinned, heat-resistant, lean desert horse. Although the Akhal-Teké has been used to upgrade other breeds, it has not had outside influences, although there was one unsuccessful attempt to outcross to the Thoroughbred. In use for hundreds of years as desert animals, the horses were wrapped in felt to protect them from the fierce heat in the day and the extreme cold at night. Although the Akhal-Teké has some conformational defects, the breed is possessed of great stamina and endurance and can exist on meager rations. It is a versatile horse, used for racing, long-distance riding, and for dressage and jumping. One particular feature of the breed is its "metallic" chestnut coloring.

Alter-Real

height *15–16 h.h. (60.2–64.2 ins; 153–163 cm)*
color *bay, brown, gray*
conformation *small head; straight or convex profile; muscular neck; strong shoulders; short, compact body; low-set tail; deep through girth*

The Alter-Real was established in Portugal in 1748 and moved to the place from which it takes its name, Alter, in 1756. The breed derives from the Andalusian *(40)*—300 mares of that breed were imported to Alter with the aim of producing quality horses to perform *haute école* (classical school riding). Although the breed flourished, it suffered great losses at the beginning of the 19th century as a result of the Peninsula wars, when the stud was sacked by French invaders and the stock was dispersed. Eventually the Royal Stud was closed. Although there were attempts to resurrect the breed in the latter part of the 19th century, it suffered from the introduction of foreign blood, mainly Hanoverian, Norman, and English. Later a massive infusion of Arab blood proved disastrous. It was only when new Andalusian blood was reintroduced at the end of the 19th century that the breed began to improve. Disaster struck again with the fall of the Portuguese monarchy in 1910 and the breed once more faced extinction. This time it was saved by the Andrade family, who retained a small number of Alter-Reals. In the 1930s the stud was passed over to the Ministry of Agriculture. The Alter-Real is tough and courageous; it displays a particularly showy action that is well suited to *haute école.*

American Quarter Horse

height *15–16 h.h. (60.2–64.2 ins; 153–163 cm)*
color *all solid colors*
conformation *short, wide head; long neck; strong shoulders; compact body; strong chest; deep girth; powerful loins; deep, well-muscled quarters; good limbs*

The American Quarter Horse was developed in Virginia in the early 17th century. It was based on English Thoroughbred (66) horses that had been imported into the country, together with Spanish stock. Its inherent versatility made it suitable for farm work and herding cattle, as well as for use in harness and riding. The Quarter Horse takes its name from the sport of racing quarter-mile distances, at which it excelled. Early examples of the breed had massive quarters that gave them the ability to sprint virtually from a standstill over short distances. The modern Quarter Horse has seen the introduction of more Thoroughbred blood. This has led to smaller quarters to improve racing speed. The Quarter Horse is very popular and its register is said to be one of the largest in the world. It is used in all forms of Western and trail riding but is also increasingly seen, once more, racing over short distances.

below: The impressive profile of an American Saddlebred is made for showing.

American Saddlebred

height *15–16 h.h. (60.2–64.2 ins; 153–163 cm)*
color *all solid colors*
conformation *quality head; large eyes; long, arched neck; sloping shoulders; short, strong back; well-sprung ribs; well-muscled quarters; high-set tail; elegant limbs; sloping pasterns; sound feet*

Originating in the southern states of America, the American Saddlebred, formerly known as the Kentucky Saddler, evolved from the old Narragansett Pacer and the Canadian Pacer. It was subsequently refined by the use of Thoroughbred (60) and Morgan (59) blood. The result is an attractive horse with active paces giving an extremely comfortable ride. The American Saddlebred is also well-suited to harness work. It is an intelligent horse with an amiable disposition and combines speed with natural balance. The horses are shown in the ring as three- or five-gaited (depending on the number of paces they employ). A horse that performs the walk, trot, and canter with a high, elevated action is described as three-gaited; a five-gaited horse achieves, in addition, the four-beat slow gait and the fast "rack." The Saddlebred is a good all-around mount possessing great stamina and a good jumping ability. It is, however, most often seen in the show ring where its naturally impressive action is heightened by growing the hooves very long and using heavy shoes.

left: The Quarter Horse takes its name from the sport of racing quarter-mile distances, at which it excelled.

American Standardbred

height *15–16 h.h.*
(60.2–64.2 ins; 153–163 cm)
color *bay, brown, chestnut*
conformation *plain head; long body; deep girth; long, sloping shoulders; croup higher than withers; strong limbs; sound feet*

The Standardbred (not pictured) is based on an English Thoroughbred called Messenger, who was imported to North America in 1788. The foundation sire of the breed is Messenger's great-grandson, Hambletonian 10, who sired more than a thousand offspring. The particular conformation of the breed is the high croup, which gives enormous thrust to the quarters. This makes it particularly suited to the sport of harness racing, which is hugely popular in many countries, especially the United States. The breed gained its name in 1879, when a speed standard was set for entry into the register of trotters. Standardbreds race at the trot or the pace, a lateral gait marginally faster than the trot. Pacers are generally more popular in the United States, but trotters are seen all over Europe.

Andalusian

height *15.2 h.h. (62.2 ins; 158 cm)*
color *gray, bay*
conformation *handsome head; fairly short, muscular neck; well-sloped shoulders; well-defined withers; strong body; rounded quarters; good joints and bones; hard feet*

The Andalusian breed evolved from the Spanish Horse. Along with the Arab *(42)* and the Barb *(42)*, the Spanish Horse has had huge influence on breeds worldwide. It is the foundation stock for most American breeds, as well as for the famous Lipizzaner *(57)*. The Andalusian may also have connections to the Barb and Sorraia, from which the Spanish Horse is said to have derived. The centers of breeding are at Jerez de la Frontera, Córdoba, and Seville in Spain. Despite its relatively diminutive size, the Andalusian has enormous presence and athletic paces. While not built for speed, the breed is very agile and is used in the bull ring and for performing *haute école*. It has a willing and equable temperament and makes an excellent all-purpose mount.

Anglo-Arab

height *15.3–16.3 h.h.*
(63.4–67.7 ins; 161–171 cm)
color *chestnut, bay, brown*
conformation *straight profile; alert ears; long neck; sloping shoulders; sound, long limbs; dense bone; well-shaped feet*

The Anglo-Arab originated in Britain and is the result of mixing Arab and Thoroughbred blood. The breed combines the stamina and inherent soundness of the former with the speed of the latter. The Anglo-Arab is now bred on a large scale in France. It traces back to two eastern sires and three Thoroughbred mares, and entry to the stud book is limited to horses with a minimum of 25 percent Arab blood. While the French Anglo-Arab has enjoyed great success in competitive equestrian spheres, it has also influenced the development of the popular sports horse, the Selle Français *(64)*. The breed is tough, versatile, and sturdier in build than a Thoroughbred.

Appaloosa

height *14.2–15.2 h.h.*
(58.25–62.2 ins; 148–158 cm)
color *spotted: blanket, marble, leopard, snowflake, frost*
conformation *refined head; mottled skin on nose; short, strong back; powerful quarters; deep girth; well-sprung ribs; good limbs; hard feet with vertical stripes*

The Appaloosa originated in north-east Oregon, southeast Washington, and the Idaho lands of North America. It was developed during the 18th century by the Nez Percé Indians, who based the breed on Spanish stock, which included a number of spotted strains. The Nez Percé practiced a strict selection process that resulted in an attractive and practical work horse. In the 1870s the Indian tribe and their horses were almost wiped out by U.S. troops, and it wasn't until the 1930s that the breed was revived and the

left: *The Andalusian is the foundation stock for most American breeds, as well as the Lipizzaner.*

Appaloosa Horse Club established. The Appaloosa has a good temperament and is a versatile breed. It is used for all types of Western riding, for endurance, and as an all-around riding horse. It is also popular outside the United States. There are five main types of Appaloosa coats: leopard (white over loins and hips with dark spots); snowflake (light spots over a dark body); blanket (white area over hips with or without dark spots); marble (mottled all over); and frost (white speckling on a dark background).

top: *The Appaloosa was developed during the 18th century by the Nez Percé Indians.*

right: *Arab and Thoroughbred blood mix in the noble Anglo-Arab, which, despite its name, is also bred in France.*

left: *The Arabian—king among horses—is the most pure of all breeds and is the fountainhead of all the world's breeds.*

Arabian

height 14.2–15 h.h.
(58.25–60.2 ins; 148–153 cm)
color *all solid colors*
conformation *dished profile with small muzzle; widely spaced, large eyes; graceful, curving neck; sloped shoulders; withers not prominent; short, strong back; deep girth; high-set tail; hard, clean limbs; well-shaped feet; silky mane and tail*

A race of horses of Arab type is thought to have existed on the Arabian Peninsula from at least 2,000–3,000 years B.C. The Arab is the purest and most beautiful of all equine breeds. Its genetic purity means that, for breeding purposes, the Arab is prepotent, stamping its powerful character on its progeny. It is the fountainhead of all the world's breeds and acknowledged as the principal foundation of the Thoroughbred. As a result of its harsh environment, the Arab is sound and enduring, with enormous stamina, and can thrive on meager rations. Bred throughout the world, the Arab is distinctive in appearance and, though fiery and courageous, it is also extremely gentle. It excels at the sport of endurance riding and is used for racing, but it also makes a popular all-around riding horse.

Australian Stock Horse (Waler)

height *15–16 h.h. (60.2–64.2 ins; 153–163 cm)*
color *all solid colors*
conformation *Thoroughbred-type head; strong neck; well-made back; well-sloped shoulders; deep chest; strong quarters; low-set joints; hard feet*

The modern Australian Stock Horse was developed from Waler stock in Australia, which in turn descended from the first horses imported into the country. These were mainly from South Africa and probably brought the infusion of Arab and Thoroughbred *(66)* blood. The Waler—named after the area of New South Wales where these horses were mainly bred—was renowned as one of the best cavalry horses. It had immense stamina, strength, and agility, and showed good resistance to heat. However, the Waler's deployment as a cavalry mount led to a drastic decline in numbers. Walers were used to found the modern Australian Stock Horse. The result shows more Thoroughbred influence than Waler, and is not yet a fixed type. It is a practical, all-around mount, with great stamina and endurance. The Australian Stock Horse has an even temper and is extremely agile, displaying the good limbs and natural balance of the Thoroughbred.

Barb

height *15.2 h.h. (62.2 ins; 158 cm)*
color *all solid*
conformation *long, plain head; straight profile; narrow skull; straight shoulders; fairly flat withers; strong body; deep girth; hard limbs; narrow, hard feet*

The Barb originates from the Barbary Coast of Morocco, and is second only to the Arab as one of the founding breeds of the world's horse population. There is no documentation to verify the Barb's origins, although one school of thought is that it may have derived from a group of wild horses that survived the Ice Age. If so, this would make it an even older breed than the Arab. As with the Arab, the spread of Barb blood was a result of Muslim conquest. The Barb has none of the Arab's visual appeal and is generally less refined, although there has been improvement to the traditional Barb in more recent times. However, it shares

the Arab's boundless stamina and endurance, and its ability to exist on meager rations. It is surefooted, agile, and very fast over short distances.

Bavarian Warmblood

height *16 h.h. (64.2 ins; 163 cm)*
color *chestnut*
conformation *quality head; strongly built; deep through the girth; short, strong legs; sound feet*

One of the oldest, though not the best known, of the German Warmbloods, the Bavarian evolved from a warhorse used during the time of the Crusades. The breed was originally known as the Rottaler because it originated in the German Rott Valley. A system of breeding was developed in monastic studs during the 16th century and 200 years later the stock was upgraded by the use of English half-breds and Cleveland Bays *(45)*, together with some Norman infusions. During the 19th century, Oldenburg blood was introduced to give substance to the stock. Later introduction of Thoroughbred *(66)* blood produced a somewhat lighter

version of the Rottaler. The modern Bavarian is an attractive horse that retains its ancestors' traditional chestnut coloring. It has a steady temperament and is a useful competition horse, particularly suited to dressage and show jumping.

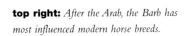

top right: *After the Arab, the Barb has most influenced modern horse breeds.*

left: *The Australian Stock Horse, a practical all-around mount, with stamina and endurance.*

right: *Evolved from the great German warhorses of the Crusades, the Bavarian Warmblood has had many infusions of cross-breeding.*

43

Budenny

height *16 h.h. (64.2 ins; 163 cm)*
color *all solid colors*
conformation *fine head and neck; short shoulders; high withers; short, straight back; small leg joints; weak hind legs; well-formed feet*

The Budenny was developed in the 1920s as part of the Soviet Union's specific breeding scheme to create improved riding horse breeds. Originally intended as a cavalry mount, the Budenny was based on Chernomor and Don *(47)* mares crossed with Thoroughbred *(66)* stallions. The breed was performance-tested and the mares that resulted from the initial scheme were put to Anglo-Don stallions, with Thoroughbred blood added where

necessary. The combination of the hardy Don and the refined Thoroughbred resulted in the tough and agile Budenny. The breed is renowned for its powers of endurance and has both jumping and racing abilities. The Budenny is fairly lightly built and, despite the fact that the limbs and joints sometimes reflect the quality of the base stock, is a tough performer.

above: *Known as the "white horse of the sea," the Camargue is used to work the wild bulls of the region.*

Camargue

height *14.2 h.h. (58.25 ins; 148 cm)*
color *gray*
conformation *coarse, heavy head; short neck; upright shoulders; powerful quarters; sloping croup; strong legs; hard feet*

Despite its small size, the Camargue is known as the "white horse of the sea." It originates in the Rhône delta in southern France. It is possible that the breed dates back to prehistoric times, as the horses are somewhat similar to the animals depicted in primitive drawings of around 15,000 B.C. in the caves at Lascaux. Apart from the initial influence of Barbs *(42)*, the breed has remained remarkably free of outside influences because of the isolation of its native terrain. Semi-wild herds (or manades) of these horses still exist in the marshlands between the town of Aigues-Mortes and the sea. Camargue cowboys use these horses for working the wild bulls of the region. The Camargue is a strong and

left: *The Cleveland Bay, the oldest and purest of British native horse breeds.*

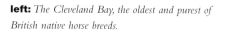

courageous breed, hardy and tough and able to exist on limited vegetation. The action of this horse shows freedom at walk, canter, and gallop, but it has a markedly stilted trot.

Canadian Cutting Horse

height *15.2–16.1 h.h.*
(62.2–64.4 ins; 158–163.5 cm)
color *all solid colors*
conformation *sensible head, strong neck; compact body; strong quarters and good limbs*

The Canadian Cutting Horse is basically Canada's version of the phenomenally popular American Quarter Horse. It is a natural cattle horse, displaying innate "cow sense," particularly at "cutting," i.e., separating specific cattle from a herd, hence its name.

It closely resembles the Quarter Horse, having a strong, flexible neck, compact body, well-muscled hindquarters, and good, strong limbs.

Cleveland Bay

height *16.2 h.h. (66.1 ins; 168 cm)*
color *bay*
conformation *bold head; large ears; strong neck; muscular shoulders; deep body; powerful quarters; clean limbs; no feathering; sound feet*

The Cleveland Bay—named after the area of Britain in which it was bred—evolved during the 17th century from the bay-colored Chapman horse with infusions of Spanish and Barb *(42)* blood. The result is a fine coach horse with active paces and the necessary stamina. When British roads improved toward the end of the 18th century, some Thoroughbred *(66)* blood was introduced into the stock to produce a faster, lighter type of animal known as the Yorkshire Coach Horse. This breed died out during the 1930s, when the motorized vehicle became the most popular method of transport. The oldest

above: *From Arab/Barb forebears, Colorado Rangers are strong workhorses that display many unusual markings.*

and purest of British native breeds, the Cleveland Bay has survived, although it has been on the Rare Breeds Trust critical list because of a lack of purebred mares. The breed is long-lived and hardy, with straight, free action. In addition to doing well in harness, the Cleveland Bay makes a good hunter.

Colorado Ranger

height *15.2 h.h. (62.2 ins; 158 cm)*
color *spotted*
conformation *refined head; deep, compact body; sound limbs; strong quarters; well-made feet*

The Colorado Ranger is based on two stallions that were presented to General Ulysses Grant by the Sultan Abdul Hamid II of Turkey in 1878. One was a purebred Arab *(42)* called Leopard, the second a Barb *(42)* stallion named Linden. Originally used to breed light harness horses in Virginia, these two stallions spent part of their later lives siring stock of native mares from Nebraska, many of which were spotted or colored. The resulting stock, which combined overall refinement with an attractive coat, became popular with Western

breeders. One of these breeders, Mike Ruby, founded what is now known as the Colorado Ranger, using two stallions tracing back to Leopard. The resulting progeny display a lot of unusual coat colorings; many of the breed display attractive patterns. The breed is an excellent workhorse, combining stamina and strength with the refinement of its Arab/Barb ancestry.

below: *The lightly built but tough and agile Budenny.*

Criollo

height *14–15 h.h. (56.3–60.2 ins; 143–153 cm)*
color *dun*
conformation *medium-sized head; muscular neck; deep body; well-sprung ribs; strong limbs; sound feet*

The Criollo (not pictured) originated in Argentina and derives from Spanish stock with a significant amount of Barb *(42)* blood. The forebears of this horse were imported to Argentina as early as 1535 A.D. by the Spanish conquistadors. The Criollo (literally "of Spanish stock") exists in other South American countries under different names—in Brazil it is known as the Crioulo, in Chile as the Caballo Chileno, and in Venezuela it's the Llanero. The Criollo has adapted to extremes of temperature—baking hot summers and severe winters—and is therefore one of the toughest of horse breeds. It was used as both a riding horse and a pack animal by earlier settlers, and today is the mount of the gaucho, the Argentinian cowboy. The breed has immense stamina and strength and is inherently sound. It is also known for its longevity. The Criollo has also had an enormous influence on the creation of the Argentinian Polo Pony.

Danish Warmblood

height *15.3–16.3 h.h. (63.4–67.3 ins; 161–171 cm)*
color *all solid colors*
conformation *quality head; long neck; well-sloped shoulders; prominent withers; muscular back; strong limbs; long forearms; correct feet*

The Danes have a long history of horse breeding stretching back to the 14th century, but it wasn't until the 1960s that the country opened a stud book for its own riding horse, the Danish Warmblood. The breed is based on the country's riding horse, the Frederiksborg *(49)*, crossed with Thoroughbred *(66)*. The resultant half-bred mares were put to Anglo-Norman (Selle-Français *(64)*), Thoroughbred, and Trakehner *(66)* stallions. Judicious selection was then used to produce a sound horse with substance, strength, good limbs, and galloping ability. Stringent grading is in place for both stallions and mares for entry into the stud book, and the best examples of the breed have a definite Thoroughbred outline combined with spirit and a good temperament. This relative latecomer to the growing band of European competition horses has proved its worth in the dressage field and other competitive spheres, including show jumping and eventing.

Døle Gudbrandsdal

height *14.2–15.2 h.h. (58.25–62.2 ins; 148–158 cm)*
color *black, brown*
conformation *pony head; straight profile; long neck; deep girth; muscular quarters; powerful hock joints; large, flat knees*

right: *The Danish Warmblood has proved its worth in the competitive disciplines of show jumping, dressage, and eventing.*

Like the British native ponies, the Fell and the Dales, which it resembles, Norway's Døle Gudbrandsdal originates from the primitive Forest Horse. Originally bred in Norway's Gudbrandsdal Valley, this horse was used as a pack and light agricultural worker. The Døle Gudbrandsdal is a compact, well-made, and hardy breed with great weight-carrying ability. It has a naturally active trot that was capitalized on to produce the Døle Trotter in the 19th century. The Døle Trotter was developed through the introduction of Thoroughbred blood, by the British stallion Odin, imported to Norway in 1834.

Don

height *15.3 h.h. (63.4 ins; 161 cm)*
color *chestnut, brown*
conformation *medium-sized head; short, straight shoulders; strong body; broad, straight back; sloping quarters; well-muscled forelimbs; upright pasterns*

The Don is traditionally associated with the Cossack cavalry. It was based on a mix of Steppe-bred Mongolian horses and swift, heat-resistant Akhal-Tekés *(38)* and Persian Arabs. Later, Orlovs *(61)*, Thoroughbreds *(66)*, and part-bred Arabs were used to upgrade the breed, but since the beginning of the 20th century there has been little outside influence. Traditionally reared in herds, the Don has evolved into a tough breed, capable of existing on meager rations. It is versatile and good-natured and is now used as a general-purpose riding horse. It has had a major influence on the creation of the Budenny *(44)*. Some conformational defects such as sickle hocks, calf knees, upright pasterns, and short, straight shoulders lead to a restricted action, but the Don's exceptional hardiness makes it a good endurance horse.

top left: *The Døle Gudbrandsdal is a compact and hardy breed, displaying a naturally active trot.*

left: *The Don—exceptional hardiness and good temperament make it an ideal all-around riding horse.*

Dutch Warmblood

height *16 h.h. (64.3 ins; 163 cm)*
color *all solid colors*
conformation *plain head; strong neck and shoulders; fairly long, but strong body; deep girth; powerful quarters; sound limbs; adequate bone; good feet*

The Dutch Warmblood (not pictured) was created by amalgamating two of Holland's native breeds, the Gelderland and the Groningen *(52)*. The former has the good movement of a carriage horse and the latter has powerful quarters for jumping. This base was then refined by the addition of Thoroughbred blood; later outcrosses were made to both German and French warmbloods to produce an athletic horse with straight action and good limbs. The Dutch Warmblood is a successful performer in the competition sphere, especially in show jumping, dressage, and carriage driving. The success of the breed is maintained by Holland's performance-based selection system, centered on physical assessment and performance tests, including show jumping, cross-country, and driving.

Einsiedler (Swiss Warmblood)

height *16.2 h.h. (66.1 ins; 168 cm)*
color *all solid colors*
conformation *fine head; broad, deep chest; long, slender legs; large, flat joints; well-formed feet of hard horn*

Originating in the 10th century and based on native Schwyer stock, the Einsiedler was first bred at the Einsiedeln monastery near Lucerne, Switzerland. After initial outcrossings to Spanish, Italian, Friesian, and Turkish stallions, the breed was improved during

above: *Fast, agile, and powerful, the Finnish is popular in harness or under saddle.*

the 19th century with the introduction of Anglo-Norman mares and a Yorkshire Coach Horse stallion. Later still, outcrosses were made to Holsteiners *(54)* and Normans. The breed, which is now known as the Swiss Warmblood, saw an introduction of Swedish and Irish mares in the 1960s, together with a variety of stallions, including Anglo-Norman, Holstein *(54)*, and Swedish. The Swiss Warmblood is now raised at the Federal Stud at Avenches. The breed undergoes strict selection and testing processes—correct conformation is paramount. It is a substantial, well-made horse with a calm temperament, and is useful in both ridden and driven disciplines.

Finnish

height *15.2 h.h. (62.2 ins; 158 cm)*
color *all solid colors*
conformation *workmanlike head; straight back; strong shoulders; sloping quarters; clean legs with little or no feathering; correct limbs*

Originally there were two types of Finnish horse: the Finnish Draft, and the lighter, more versatile Finnish Universal, which could be ridden or used in harness. The former—

below: *Substantial and well made, the Einsiedler has proved itself as a useful competition horse.*

powerfully built but with quick paces—was suited to agricultural and forestry work. The breeds originated from native Finnish pony breeds crossed with both cold- and warm-blooded horses, especially the Oldenburger. In 1907 the opening of a stud book for both strains instigated rigorous performance testing. Although there is still a need for the heavier type of horse, the emphasis has been on the lighter type, which is a popular harness horse and ridden mount. The modern breed of Finnish Horse has quite a small frame and is fast and agile, as well as very powerful. It is long-lived and enduring, with an excellent constitution and great stamina.

Frederiksborg

height *15.3 h.h. (63.4 ins; 161 cm)*
color *chestnut*
conformation *plain head; short, upright neck; upright shoulders; fairly long but strong back; flat withers; strong feet*

Originating in Denmark, the Frederiksborg was bred at the Royal Frederiksborg Stud, founded in 1562. The origins of the breed were based on Andalusian *(40)* horses imported from Spain. Later on, Neapolitan stock was introduced and later still outcrosses were made to half-bred English stallions. The breed was extremely popular as a spirited and elegant saddle horse, military charger, and a means of upgrading other stock, including the Danish Heavy Horse, the Jutland. Gradually the number of Frederiksborgs became depleted and, in the late 1830s, the stud turned to Thoroughbred breeding. The Frederiksborg was in danger of dying out but a number of individuals continued to breed it. As the demand for smart riding horses increased, more Thoroughbred blood was introduced. The Frederiksborg has a high, vigorous action and an equable temperament. It has been used to develop the popular competition horse, the Danish Warmblood.

below: *Because of its unusually high action, the Frederiksborg was popular among "heroic" military men for showing them off. The modern horse is lighter, with more Thoroughbred blood.*

Freiberger (Franches Montagne)

height *15 h.h. (60.2 ins; 153 cm)*
color *all solid colors*
conformation *short, strong neck; compact body; well-muscled quarters; well-developed second thigh; short, strong legs*

Originating in the Jura region of western Switzerland, the Freiberger (not pictured), or Franches Montagne as it is also known, is a mountain-bred horse. There are strong Norman connections with many of the breed. These can be traced back to a stallion called Valliant, foaled in 1891, who through his sire has Norfolk connections and through his granddam traces back to Anglo-Norman stock. In later years there were outcrosses made to French, English, and Belgian horses, but it wasn't until the mid-1940s that a new bloodline emerged through the stallion Urus, who also had strong Norman connections. Breeding has since become more selective, with mainly Anglo-Norman but also some Arab blood used. The Frieberger has the build of a heavy cob and is sure-footed, active, and good-natured. Used as a pack horse by the Swiss Army, the Frieberger is also useful working on mountain farms and in harness.

French Trotter

height *up to 16.2 h.h. (66.1 ins; 168 cm)*
color *all solid colors*
conformation *well-sloped shoulders; flat withers; powerful quarters; strong body; strong limbs and feet*

The French Trotter evolved during the 19th century as a result of crossing the Norman horse with English Thoroughbreds, half-breds, and Norfolk Roadsters. The Thoroughbreds *(66)* gave the breed speed and stamina and the Norfolk Roadsters contributed to its trotting ability. Later infusions of American Standardbred *(40)* blood increased its general speed. France has a great tradition of trotting races, both ridden and harness. The first ridden race was recorded in the early 1800s, and the sport has increased in popularity ever since. The French Trotter is a large, tough breed. The bigger animals are still raced under saddle.

Friesian

height *15–16 h.h. (60.2–64.2 ins; 153–163 cm)*
color *black*
conformation *long head; short ears; arched neck; strong shoulders; powerful body; strong quarters and limbs; thick feathering on heels; hard hooves of blue horn*

The Friesian is a coldblood from Friesland in the north of the Netherlands, with ancient origins dating back to the primitive Forest Horse. The main influence on the Friesian was from Andalusian *(40)* stock during the time of Spanish occupation. Later, the introduction of eastern blood upgraded the breed further and, as a result, the Friesian was in much demand to upgrade other stocks. As a consequence it has had a great influence on a number of breeds, including the Oldenburg, Døle Gudbrandsdale, Dales and Fell ponies, and the Shire horse *(72)*. Despite its high profile, the breed was in danger of dying out in the early part of the 20th century. At this time outcrosses were made to improve the speed of the Friesian's high-stepping trot, but they were made at the expense of essential type and the Friesian became lighter in build. However, there was renewed interest in this lovely natured and robust breed in the second half of the 20th century. It is a particularly versatile animal, both as an agile mount and an excellent carriage horse.

Furioso

height *16 h.h. (64.2 ins; 163 cm)*
color *black, brown*
conformation *fine head; compact body; well-sloped shoulders; compact body; deep girth; strong hind legs*

Closely related to the Nonius *(60)*, the Furioso was developed at Hungary's famous Mezöhegyes Stud by putting English Thoroughbreds to local Nonius mares. Two stallions,

left: *Strong limbs and feet make the French Trotter a prized racehorse.*

Furioso and North Star, were imported to Hungary during the 1840s. The latter, a son of the 1834 St. Leger winner Touchstone, had Norfolk Roadster connections that lent strength and stamina to the breed. Originally the two lines were separate, but they were merged in 1885, with the Furioso line becoming the most prominent. The breed is an excellent riding and competition horse and a popular choice of mount—sound, hardy, and intelligent. It is bred in many other countries, including Austria and Poland.

above: *The ancient Friesian has had a significant influence on many breeds.*

right: *A Furioso-North Star mare; bred from Poland to Austria, the Furioso is an excellent riding horse.*

above: *In the Gelderlander, the Dutch bred a strong carriage horse with an equable temper.*

Gelderlander

height *15.2–16.2 h.h.*
(62.2–66.1 ins; 158–168 cm)
color *chestnut*
conformation *plain head; strong neck and shoulders; fairly low withers; deep through girth; long back; strong body; short, strong limbs; powerful quarters; sound feet*

Developed in the 19th century in the Gelder province of the Netherlands, the Gelderlander is a result of crossing native mares with a number of different bloods, including Norfolk Roadster, German, Polish, Hanoverian, and Russian outcrosses. When a fixed type was established,

left: *With stronger quarters, the Groningen is heavier than the Gelderlander.*

Cleveland Bay *(45)*, Oldenburg *(61)*, and Anglo-Norman blood was added. Hackney *(52)* and Arab blood was introduced later still. The Gelderlander and Groningen are the two main bases for the sports horse, the Dutch Warmblood. The breed is an upstanding carriage horse with good shoulders giving a free action, and powerful, strong limbs. As well as competing successfully in carriage driving, the Gelderlander is a good, heavyweight horse with some jumping ability.

Groningen

height *15.2–16.2 h.h.*
(62.2–66.1 ins; 158–168 cm)
color *bay, brown*
conformation *plain head; long body and back; strong neck; strong quarters; deep girth; ample bone*

This breed was developed in the Groningen region of the Netherlands and originally bred as a light draft horse and coach horse. It was based on Friesians *(50)* and Oldenburgs *(61)* and was particularly noted for its strong hindquarters. The old type no longer exists, but the modern version of the

breed is a lighter, more active horse, with a calm nature and willing disposition. When crossed with quality stock, the breed passes on size and good bone, and is, with the Gelderlander, the main base for the successful competition horse, the Dutch Warmblood.

Hackney Horse

height *15–15.2 h.h.*
(60.2–62.2 ins; 153–158 cm)
color *dark brown, black, bay, or chestnut*
conformation *neat head; long, well-formed neck; deep chest; low withers; compact body; maximum flexion in hock joints; well-shaped feet*

Deriving from Norfolk and Yorkshire Roadsters, the Hackney Horse is prized for its high-stepping, flamboyant action. Developed in the 18th century, the Hackney is a descendant of the renowned English trotting horses, the Norfolk and Yorkshire Trotters. These share a common ancestry in Shales, the son of Blaze, a Thoroughbred. Blaze was the son of one of the first great racehorses, Flying Childers, and a grandson of The Darley Arabian, one of the foundation sires of the Thoroughbred. Thus the Hackney has a strong Thoroughbred connection, although it is prized for its trotting rather than its galloping ability. The Hackney Horse Society was formed in 1883, and the breed is exported all over the world. It has a particularly arresting action, high and floating. The breed is most often seen in the show ring.

Hanoverian

height *15.3–16.2 h.h.*
(63.4–66.1 ins; 161–168 cm)
color *all solid colors*
conformation *clean-cut head; long, fine neck; strong back; sloping shoulders; muscular quarters; deep through the girth; powerful limbs; hard, well-formed feet*

The most famous of all the German Warmbloods, the Hanoverian was founded in 1735 with the founding of the Celle Stud by George II, Elector of Hanover and King of England. Initially, Holsteins *(54)* were used on

Hispano

height *up to 16 h.h. (64.2 ins; 163 cm)*
color *bay, chestnut, gray*
conformation *refined, Arab head; strong muscular neck; well-sloped shoulders; muscular hindquarters; strong limbs.*

The Hispano, or Spanish Anglo-Arab, as it is also known, has derived from crossing Spanish Arab mares with Thoroughbred stock. It is a popular and attractive riding horse, displaying more pronounced Arab characteristics than many other Anglo-Arab types. It combines courage and agility with a tractable disposition and in this respect is a popular choice in competitive riding.

local mares to give size and substance, but the introduction of Thoroughbreds *(66)* led to a better quality horse. Later still, the addition of Trakehner *(66)* and Thoroughbred blood helped give further refinement and the emphasis was placed on producing a competition horse. A policy of strict selection—including veterinary inspections and performance tests—has resulted in a universally popular sports horse. The Hanoverian is strong and athletic, with correct movement and a willing temperament. It particularly excels at dressage and show jumping.

top: *The strong and athletic Hanoverian is probably the most successful of all competition horses.*

above: *With its high-stepping action, the Hackney is the world's most flamboyant carriage horse.*

Holstein

height *16–17 h.h. (60.2–68.1 ins; 163–173 cm)*
color *all solid colors*
conformation *expressive head; large eyes; long, slightly arched neck; pronounced withers; strong body; muscular loins; correct limbs; strong quarters; good, hard feet*

Dating from the 17th century, the early Holstein was a popular coach horse with a mixture of German, Spanish, and Eastern blood. Two factors were an important influence in the production of the modern Holstein. The first took place during the 19th century, when the Yorkshire Coach Horse was introduced to upgrade the breed, lending it substance, strength, and action. The second occurred later, when Thoroughbred *(66)* blood was used to add refinement and speed. The further use of Thoroughbred blood has resulted in a lighter competition horse with a greater range. The breed shows correct paces, a good temperament, and boldness. It makes an excellent dressage, show jumping, or eventing horse, and competes successfully in carriage-driving races.

Irish Draft

height *mares 15.2 h.h.*
(62.2 ins; 158 cm) upward;
stallions 16.2 h.h. (66.1 ins; 168 cm) upward
color *all solid colors*
conformation *intelligent head; sloping shoulders; strong body; deep chest; strong limbs; well-made, sound feet*

The Irish Draft has evolved from native stock; its size was increased by the influence of French, and probably Flemish, heavy horses during the 12th century and later refined by the infusion of Spanish blood. After showing signs of a serious decline in numbers during the mid-19th century, the modern breed has survived as a result of government subsidies introduced for approved stallions of Irish Draft and hunter type. The Irish Draft Society was formed in 1976. Crossing the Irish Draft with a Thoroughbred makes

above: *Although retaining the heavy limbs of its ancestors, the modern Irish Draft is very athletic, and has an equable temperament.*

right: *The Karabair is quick and agile, and the breed is performance-tested on the racetrack.*

one of the best horses across country, the Irish Hunter. The breed is naturally hardy, has a natural athletic jump, an equable disposition, and is easy to manage.

Kabardin

height *15–15.2 h.h.*
(60.2–62.2 ins; 153–158 cm)
color *bay, black*
conformation *long head; medium-length neck; straight shoulders; short, straight back; strong limbs; sickle-shaped hind legs over hocks; strong feet*

This tough mountain horse developed in the northern Caucasus during the 16th century as a result of crossing steppe-bred horses with Persian, Turkmene, and Karabakh *(56)* strains. The breed has been upgraded by selective breeding, and the Kabardin itself is used to upgrade neighboring stock. Originally rather small, it has developed as a tough, sturdy mountain breed, possessing great powers of endurance.

The breed declined in numbers during the Russian Revolution, but it was later reestablished as a larger stamp of horse suitable both as an army remount and for light draft work. The modern horse is ridden or used in harness.

When crossed to Thoroughbreds, it results in a bigger, faster animal that retains its natural hardiness.

Karabair

height *15 h.h. (60.2 ins; 153 cm)*
color *chestnut, bay, gray*
conformation *fine head; straight profile; straight neck; wide chest; well-sprung ribs; short, muscular back; well-developed quarters; long hind legs; strong, fine legs; hard joints; strong feet*

The Karabair originated in Uzbekskaya and derives from crossing oriental breeds with steppe horses of primitive type. Although it is coarser and less refined than the Arab, it is a quick and agile horse possessing great endurance. The breed is inherently sound and has developed into a dual-purpose horse of quality and with reasonably good conformation. The Karabairs are still traditionally bred in herds and are performance-tested on the racecourse at two and three years old.

left: *A true mountain-bred horse, the Kabardin is naturally hardy, and capable of negotiating treacherous terrain with agility.*

above: *The old Knabstrup was popular as a performing horse in circuses. The modern examples are substantial in build with colorings similar to the Appaloosa.*

Karabakh

height *14 h.h. (56.3 ins; 143 cm)*
color *chestnut, bay, dun*
conformation *refined head showing Arab influence, arched neck; upright shoulders; slender legs; small joints; hard-wearing feet*

Originating from the Karabakh uplands of Azerbaijan, the breed (not pictured) has strong Eastern connections, having been heavily influenced by the Arab as well as other Oriental breeds, including the Akhal-Teké. It is from the latter that the Karabakh has inherited its striking metallic sheen.

The breed is essentially a working mountain breed, and while it may show conformational defects that would not be acceptable in a traditional riding horse, it is a useful mount noted for its speed and agility.

Kathiawari

height *15 h.h. (60.2 ins; 153 cm)*
color *all solid colors except black*
conformation *long, narrow head; distinctive ears that curve inward with tips touching; elegant neck; sloped shoulders; narrow body; sloping quarters; low-set tail; well-shaped, hard feet*

The Kathiawari (not pictured) descended from native Indian stock. It probably carries eastern blood from the Kabuli and Baluchi breeds, which were crossed with Arabian horses imported to India during the time of the Moghul Emperors from the 16th century onward. The horse was bred by many different noble households, and even today around 28 strains of the breed exist. The Kathiawari shows definite Arab influence, but the most distinctive feature of the breed is its long, mobile ears that curve inward and touch at the tips. Despite being light in bone, it is a very sound breed, heat-resistant, and able to survive on minimal rations. The Kathiawari's

ability to employ the lateral gait—the pace—may indicate a connection with horses of Central Asia.

Knabstrup

height *15.2 h.h. (62.2 ins; 158 cm)*
color *spotted*
conformation *intelligent head; mottled muzzle; short, strong neck; strong, broad loins; flat knees; vertical stripes on hooves*

The Knabstrup was developed during the early 19th century in Denmark. The breed was based on a spotted Spanish mare, called Flaebehoppen, which was put to a Frederiksborg stallion by her owner. The foundation sire of the breed is believed to be Mikkel, the grandson of Flaebehoppen. The original mare was particularly fast and enduring and the resulting offspring were tough, intelligent horses with tractable natures. Their attractive spotted coats made them particularly popular as circus horses. The original Knabstrup breed now only exists in small numbers; this is because the Knabstrups were bred specifically for color rather than conformation. The modern breed has similar coloring to the Appaloosa *(40)* and is fairly substantial in build. It has the mottled skin coloring on the lips and muzzle typical of all spotted horses.

Latvian

height *16 h.h. (64.2 ins; 163 cm)*
color *all solid colors but usually black or chestnut*
conformation *sensible head; strong neck; good depth of girth; sufficient bone; strong legs*

The Latvian (not pictured) is a horse of relatively recent origin, having been bred from native mares crossed with stock from Germany, France, and England to produce a useful, all-around working horse. The increased use of Hannoverian blood produced a lighter riding horse.

Both types are renowned for having generally good conformation and free action, while the heavy horse displays strength and stamina and is particularly noted for its gentle temperament.

Lipizzaner

height *15–16.2 h.h.*
(60.2–66.1 ins; 153–168 cm)
color *gray*
conformation *neat head; short, thick neck; low withers; compact body; deep girth; powerful quarters; short, powerful limbs; good bone; hard feet*

The Lipizzaner evolved at the Lipica Stud in Slovenia and was developed from Spanish horses imported by Archduke Charles II, whose aim was to breed a supply of grand white horses for the ducal stables at Graz and the court stables at Vienna. The breed is associated with the Spanish Riding School in Vienna, so called because of its use of Spanish horses from the outset. The school was set up in 1572 to instruct the nobility in classical equitation. The Spanish Riding School horses are raised at the Piber Stud in Austria, but the Lipizzaner is bred extensively in other countries, including Hungary, Romania, Czech Republic, Slovakia, and Slovenia, and each country develops its own type. Although the Lipizzaner is renowned for its gray coat, foals are born brown or black, and occasionally bay horses occur. The breed is long-lived and agile. Its athletic, powerful physique makes it ideally suited to the *haute école* movements performed at the Spanish Riding School. The Lipizzaner also makes an excellent carriage horse.

below: *The Lipizzaner has a powerful physique suited to the* haute école *movements performed at the Spanish Riding School.*

Lusitano

height *15–16 h.h. (60.2–64.2 ins; 153–163 cm)*
color *all solid colors*
conformation *long head; short, powerful neck; low withers; powerful shoulders; compact body; powerful loins; long limbs*

The Lusitano is, to all intents and purposes, a Portuguese version of the Andalusian *(40)*, although Spain and Portugal established their own separate stud books in the early part of this century. The Portuguese continue to improve the breeding program for the Lusitano and, in particular, are keen to retain the animal's strength and courage. Originally used as a mount for the Portuguese army, the Lusitano is also deployed in the bullring and in *haute école*. It is an intelligent and gentle animal showing great agility and a naturally elevated action. It has found favor in other countries, especially Britain and the United States. The breed is particularly noted for its luxuriant mane and tail.

Maremmana

height *15.3 h.h. (63.4 ins; 161 cm)*
color *all solid colors*
conformation *short, weak neck; upright shoulders; flat withers; well-defined hock and knee joints*

The Maremmana is bred in Tuscany, Italy, and is thought to have descended from the once-famous Neapolitan horses, with later outcrosses to British stock, including Norfolk Roadsters. The breed is not known for its beauty, but it is a solid, steady horse that is easy to keep and can be ridden and used for light agricultural work. The Maremmana is used by the Italian police and cavalry and is well-known as the mount of the *butteri*, the Italian cowboy. Since the 1940s the use of better-quality stallions has eradicated some of the old conformational defects and the resulting offspring have more

above: *While not particularly fast, the Maremmana is good natured and is used by the* butteri, *the Italian cowboy.*

correct limbs. Although the breed is not known for its speed, it is good-natured and willing.

left: *The Lusitano is intelligent and gentle, displaying a naturally elevated action.*

Missouri Fox Trotter

height *16 h.h. (64.2 ins; 163 cm)*
color *all colors, but mainly chestnut*
conformation *neat, plain head; graceful neck; well-sloped muscular shoulders; deep, strong body; powerful shoulders; strong limbs; sound feet*

The breed was developed in the Arkansas and Missouri regions of the United States by early settlers who interbred horses of Spanish ancestry with Morgans and Thoroughbreds (66). They later introduced Saddlebred (39) and Tennessee Walking Horse (65) blood. The result was a horse capable of traversing rough terrain for long periods. The breed owes its name to its broken gait, known as the "fox trot," whereby the horse walks quickly with its forelegs and trots with its hind legs. The result is a smooth movement that can be sustained for long periods of time. The stud book for the breed was not opened until 1948. The Missouri Fox Trotter is an all-around pleasure and show horse. It is usually ridden in Western saddle.

Morgan

height *14.2–15.2 h.h. (58.25–62.2 ins; 148–158 cm)*
color *bay, chestnut, brown, black*
conformation *straight or slightly dished profile; strong shoulders; clearly defined withers; compact body; well-formed quarters; clean joints; flat bone; round feet; dense horn on hooves*

The Morgan was developed in the late 18th century. It is unusual in that it descends from one prepotent sire, Just Morgan, named after his owner. Despite the stallion's small stature (he was only 14 hands high), he was immensely strong and excelled in weight-pulling contests. He was raced both under saddle and in harness. Although all Morgans relate back to this sire, there is little known of his own breeding; nevertheless, he passed on his qualities of strength, speed, and a gentle temperament. The Morgan is popular as a show-ring horse, but can be ridden or put to harness. The feet can be artificially shod to emphasize the horse's elevated action. However, if the feet are trimmed normally the Morgan displays a free movement. The breed is hardy, strong, and easily managed.

left: *Its unusual gait, walking quickly with the forelegs and trotting with the hind, gave the Missouri Fox Trotter its name.*

Mustang

height *13.2–15 h.h.*
(54.3–60.2 ins; 138–153 cm)
color *all colors*
conformation *varies enormously, but good examples have a head showing its Spanish ancestry; strong body; strong, clean limbs; hard feet*

The name Mustang comes from the Spanish *mestena*, meaning "herd." The breed originates from Spanish horses brought to America in the 16th century. Many of these horses strayed or were turned loose and became feral, thus forming the beginnings of herds that spread across North America. At the beginning of the 20th century there were believed to be more than one million wild horses in the western United States. By the 1970s, numbers had declined drastically as horses were killed for meat. In 1971 the wild Mustang was given protection by law, and there are now a number of places in the United States where the breed exists in its natural state. If

domesticated, the Mustang can make a good general-purpose horse. It is agile and fast, and some of the breed still retain the strength and physical characteristics of their Spanish forebears.

Nonius

height 15.3–16.2 h.h.
(63.4–66.1 ins; 161–168 cm)
color bay, brown
conformation straight profile; sloping shoulders;
strong back; strong quarters; hard feet

Closely related to but more heavily built than the Furioso (50), the Nonius was developed at the Mezöhegyes Stud in Hungary during the 19th century. The foundation sire of the breed was the Anglo-Norman Nonius Senior, reputedly by the English half-bred Orion out of a Norman mare. Nonius Senior was a successful sire, producing good quality stock from a variety of breeds, including Arab, Lipizzaner, Norman, and English mares. The resulting progeny were then mated back to him. Later, more Thoroughbred blood was introduced and the breed divided into two distinct types: the larger, light farm worker, and the lighter riding type. The former has become popular in carriage driving, a sport at which the Hungarians excel, while the saddle type is a useful all-around mount. The breed is long-lived and, although not fast, has active paces and a willing disposition.

Oldenburg

height 16–17 h.h. (64.2–68.1 ins; 163–173 cm)
color all solid
conformation straight profile; strong neck;
powerful body; strong hindquarters; large joints

The Oldenburg evolved in the early 17th century from Friesian stock (50), and takes its name from Count Anton Gunther von Oldenburg. The count was largely instrumental in developing the breed as a good, strong coach horse. Gradually Spanish and Neapolitan blood, and later English half-bred stallions, were introduced. At the end of the 19th century Thoroughbred, Cleveland Bay (45), and Norman blood was introduced, then, later still, Hanoverian (53). The breeding program of the Oldenburg has been skillfully controlled to produce a horse that meets the requirements of a changing world. When once the Oldenburg was used for agricultural work, it is now in demand as a competition horse, particularly suited to dressage and carriage driving. It is the heaviest of all the German Warmbloods and—although the Thoroughbred influence has largely eliminated its former coach horse characteristics, with exceptions that still have a high knee action—it has correct, rhythmic paces.

Orlov Trotter

height 16 h.h. (64.2 ins; 163 cm)
color gray, bay, black
conformation small, sometimes coarse head; long neck, set high on shoulders; low withers; long body; powerful croup; long limbs

The Orlov Trotter was founded in the 18th century at the Khrenov Stud, near Moscow, by Count Alexis Orlov. The Count used an Arab stallion called Smetanka on a variety of mares. The foundation sire of the breed, Bars I, was by Polkan I, a direct descendent of Smetanka out of a Dutch mare. Bars I was mated with Arab, Dutch, Danish, and English half-breds. The fixed type was obtained by inbreeding to the foundation horse. The breed continued to improve and become faster with the training and racing of trotters in Russia. However, with the rise of the Standardbred, the Orlov was frequently crossed with horses imported from the United States; this cross produced the faster racing horse, the Russian Trotter (63). The Orlov is a tall, well-muscled, lightly built horse. It is also well suited to carriage driving.

top: While not as swift as some of the other harness breeds, the Orlov Trotter is still popular in its homeland.

right: The Oldenburg is not built for speed, but has correct, rhythmic paces suitable for show-jumping and dressage.

and Hucul stock in maintained herds in Poland; the Tundra; and the Forest Horse. The Przewalski's Horse *(Equus przewalskii przewalskii poliakof)*, or the Asian Wild Horse, no longer exists in the wild but is preserved in zoos around the world. The horse gained its name from a colonel in the Russian army, N. M. Przewalski, who discovered a herd of wild horses in Mongolia in 1881. A truly wild animal, which has had no attempts at domestication made upon it, the Przewalski's Horse is remarkably tough and enduring, capable of existing on the poorest of vegetation and withstanding extreme weather conditions. It displays primitive characteristics such as an upright mane, dun coloring, and a pronounced dorsal eel stripe. And while the domestic horse has 64 chromosomes, Przewalski's Horse has 66.

Peruvian Paso

height *14–15 h.h. (56.3–60.2 ins; 143–153 cm)*
color *all solid colors*
conformation *short, muscular neck; strong body; deep girth; strong quarters; short, strong limbs; good feet*

The breed derives from Spanish stock imported to South America by the conquistadors in the 16th century. The Peruvian Paso has a unique lateral gait, called the paso, and breeding has been specifically to perfect this peculiar characteristic. The paso involves vigorous movement of the forelegs, while the hind legs are driven forward with the hindquarters lowered. This pace is particularly noticeable at a canter and results in a smooth ride that can be sustained for extended periods over rough terrain. The Peruvian Paso is relatively small and stocky; it is sure-footed and tough and can exist on minimal rations.

The Paso Fino is the American-bred equivalent of the Peruvian Paso, deriving from the same Spanish root. As with its Peruvian counterpart, it is its unusual gaits—the paso fino, corto, and largo—that make the breed renowned for its smooth and exceptionally comfortable paces.

Przewalski's Horse

height *12–14.2 h.h. (48.4–58.25 ins; 123–148 cm)*
color *dun*
conformation *long, heavy head; straight profile; short neck; short, upright mane; sloping quarters; hard, flat hooves*

The only survivor of the four primitive equine horses. These include the Tarpan, which is technically extinct, although it exists in a reconstructed form bred from Konik

Salerno

height *16 h.h. (64.2 ins; 163 cm)*
color *all solid colors*
conformation *quality head; good, sloping riding shoulders; strong quarters; well-shaped legs; fine joints; good feet*

above: *Strong and athletic, the Salerno was a favorite cavalry mount, and is now a useful competition horse.*

Originating in the Campania region of Italy during the 18th century, the Salerno evolved from the Persano horse. The latter was based on the Neapolitan crossed with local horses from the Salerno and Ofanto valleys, with later infusions of Arab and Spanish blood. The result was a good quality riding horse. However, breeding died out after the Italian Republic was established in 1860 and it was not until the 1900s that breeding resumed again, at which point the type became known as the Salerno. The introduction of Thoroughbred blood produced a bigger, more attractive animal, with good conformation and action. The Salerno has been increasingly refined with the continued addition of Thoroughbred blood. With a free, athletic action and a good jump, it is a useful competition horse.

Russian Trotter

height *15.3–16 h.h. (63.4–64.2 ins; 161–163 cm)*
color *bay, black, chestnut, gray*
conformation *plain head; straight profile; trotting shoulders; deep girth; muscular legs; upright pasterns; sound feet*

The Russian Trotter was developed with the rise of harness racing in the former Soviet Union. It resulted from the desire to produce a faster version of the Orlov Trotter *(61)*, which had begun to be outclassed in the sport by the American Standardbred. The Russian Trotter is based on crossing Orlov stock with Standardbreds. The result is a smaller and less elegant animal than the Orlov, but it is faster and capable of competing on the international trotting circuit. The modern Russian Trotter, which derives from the original sporting type developed in the 1930s, is a light horse with good muscular development and hard, clean limbs. It has a long, low action and is quick to mature. Because of the popularity of the Russian Trotter abroad, more American Standardbreds were imported to the former Soviet Union in the 1970s to further improve its speed.

right: *Orlov stock was crossed with Standardbreds to produce the popular Russian Trotter.*

Selle Français

height *15.2–16.3 h.h.*
(62.2–67.3 ins; 158–171 cm)
color *all solid colors*
conformation *refined head; long, elegant neck; sloping shoulders; strong body; powerful hindquarters; strong limbs; powerful forearms; clean joints; good bone*

The Selle Français, or French Saddlebred, only came into being in the late 1950s; the stud book was established in the following decade. French breeders in the 19th century laid the foundations for the breed by importing English Thoroughbreds and half-bred stallions to cross with their useful Norman stock. The offspring were the forerunners of the French Trotter *(50)* and the Selle Français. The latter developed further after the Second World War with the addition of Trotter, Thoroughbred, Arab, and Anglo-Arab blood. This tough, agile breed is a prominent competition horse that particularly excels in show jumping, three-day eventing, and racing.

above: *The Selle Français is tough and agile and excels at show jumping and three-day eventing.*

Shagya Arabian

height *15 h.h. (60.2 ins; 153 cm)*
color *all solid colors*
conformation *refined head; wide forehead; dished profile; elegant neck; sloping shoulders; compact back; high-set tail; well-formed feet*

The Shagya Arab is a strain of Arabian horse that evolved at the Babolna Stud in Hungary and takes its name from the foundation sire, a Syrian stallion called Shagya. Mated with mares of mixed blood but distinctly Eastern in appearance, the Shagya Arab evolved as a quality riding horse and was used mainly as a cavalry mount. While completely Arab in outline and character, the Shagya is bigger and has more substance (Shagya himself was slightly larger than the average Arab). It is a popular riding horse and goes well in harness. The Shagya combines qualities of elegance and toughness, and is bred in a number of countries, including Austria, the former Yugoslavia, and Germany.

right: *Bigger than the Arab, the Shagya Arabian combines elegance with toughness and is ridden or driven.*

Swedish Warmblood

height *16.2 h.h. (66.1 ins; 168 cm)*
color *all solid colors*
conformation *handsome head; long neck; strong shoulders; compact body; well-sprung ribs; strong limbs; sound feet*

Originally developed as a cavalry mount, the Swedish Warmblood evolved from horses imported into Sweden during the 17th century, mainly Spanish and Friesian stallions; when crossed with local mares, they produced good, strong horses. In the 19th and 20th centuries, Arab,

above: *The Swedish Warmblood is versatile, proving successful in dressage, show jumping, and eventing.*

Thoroughbred *(66)*, Hanoverian *(53)*, and Trakehner blood *(66)* was introduced to produce large, imposing animals. The modern Swedish Warmblood is a sound riding horse, with straight, easy paces and a tractable nature. It is versatile, proving successful in a number of competitive disciplines, including dressage, show jumping, and eventing. To maintain the overall standard of the breed, there is a rigorous system of testing. Animals undergo veterinary, performance, and conformation checks before they are accepted for breeding.

Tchenarani

height *15 h.h. (60.2 ins; 153 cm)*
color *all solid colors*
conformation *small, refined head showing Arab influence; strong, compact body; sound limbs; hard feet*

Bred in the northern regions of Iran, the Tchenarani (not pictured) was derived from crossing Plateau horses—strains of Arab-type horses that lived on the plateaus of Iran—with Turkmene mares. Today this is

the preferred breeding strategy in order to prevent the Tchenarani from deteriorating. A wiry, agile horse, displaying Arab characteristics, the breed is tough and enduring, which made it a popular choice as a cavalry horse.

below: *One of the most comfortable rides in the world, the Tennessee Walking Horse.*

Tennessee Walking Horse

height *15–16 h.h. (60.2–64.2 ins; 153–163 cm)*
color *all solid colors*
conformation *plain head; strong, arched neck; short body; well-sloped shoulders; broad chest; strong quarters; hard limbs*

The breed developed in the 19th century as a mount for plantation owners and derives from the old Narragansett Pacer with a mix of Thoroughbred *(66)*, Standardbred, Morgan *(59)*, and American Saddlebred blood. The foundation sire of the breed is the Standardbred *(39)* trotter, Black Allan. With its three, bounce-free gaits, the Tennessee Walking Horse is said to be one of the most comfortable rides in the world. The gaits are a flat walk; a running walk, which has four beats and with which the horse nods its head in time; and the "rocking chair" canter. Although popular in the show ring, the breed's exceptionally good nature makes it a wonderful family horse.

left: *An Arabian-looking horse with good paces, the elegant Tersk is an all-around riding and competition horse.*

Tersk

height *15 h.h. (60.2 ins; 153 cm)*
color *gray*
conformation *fine head; medium-length neck; short, compact body; well-sprung ribs; well-sloped shoulders; deep chest; clean legs*

Like the Kabardin (55), the Tersk originates from the northern Caucasus. The breed was developed at the Tersk and Stavropol Studs from the 1920s to the 1950s, so it is relatively recent in origin. The breed is based upon the Strelets, which were part-bred Arabs from the Strelets Stud in the Ukraine. The Strelets were a result of crossing pure-bred Arabs with Orlovs (61) and Anglo-Arabs (40). In an attempt to reverse the decline in the number of Strelets, cross-bred mares were put to Strelets stallions and Strelet mares were put to pure-bred Arabs. In the 1960s the type became fixed and known as the Tersk. It is similar to, though slightly bigger than, the Arab, and retains that breed's elegant paces. The Tersk is very versatile, combining good paces with a natural jumping ability and boldness. It is intelligent and gentle, a popular all-around riding and competition horse.

Thoroughbred

height *16–16.2 h.h.
(64.2–66.1 ins; 163–168 cm)*
color *all solid colors*
conformation *refined head; graceful neck; long, sloping shoulders; strong body; deep through the girth; powerful hindquarters; fine limbs; flat joints; long hind legs; a minimum of 7.9 ins (20 cm) of bone below the knee*

The fastest of all horses, this valuable breed originated in Britain during the 17th and 18th centuries, when native horses, known as "running horses," used in races were crossed with oriental stallions. The foundation horses of the breed were The Byerley Turk, Darley Arabian, and Godolphin Arabian. Between them these horses produced the four principal Thoroughbred lines: Herod, Eclipse, Matchem, and Highflyer (Herod's son). The general stud book (volume I) was begun in 1880, after several preliminary editions. Probably one of the most beautiful breeds in the world, the Thoroughbred has speed, stamina and endurance in equal measure, and excels in all equestrian spheres. It is full of spirit and presence and is used to produce competition horses and upgrade other breeds.

Trakehner

height *16–17.2 h.h. (64.2–70 ins; 163–178 cm)*
color *all solid colors*
conformation *quality head; long, elegant neck; sloping shoulders; strong body; powerful quarters; strong limbs; good, hard feet*

The Trakehner originated in East Prussia around the 13th century, but came to prominence in the 1730s when the Royal Trakehner Stud was founded by Freiderich Wilhelm I of Prussia to produce good coach horses. The base of the breed was the indigenous Schweiken pony, which can be traced back to the Tarpan. At the beginning of the 19th century Thoroughbred and Arab blood were introduced to produce effective army remounts. The greatest influence on the breed was Templehunter, the Thoroughbred son of

left: *The fastest of all horses, the Thoroughbred excels in all equestrian spheres.*

above: Spirited and enduring, the Trakehner is one of Europe's foremost competition horses.

the 1896 Derby and St. Leger winner Persimmon Perfection. Templehunter provided the line that is recognized as the foundation of the modern breed. During the Second World War, the Germans used Trakehners as cavalry mounts. Thousands of horses were lost when, to escape the advancing Russian troops, German soldiers undertook a three-month trek across East Prussia. The surviving animals were eventually re-registered and breeding was resumed. The Trakehner is a spirited and enduring horse with excellent conformation. It excels at show jumping, dressage, and eventing.

Württemburg

height *16 h.h. (64.3 ins; 163 cm)*
color *brown, bay, chestnut*
conformation *bold eye; medium-length neck; correct proportions; broad loins; sound limbs; strong bone; strong feet*

The Württemburg (not pictured) evolved during the 17th century at the oldest of Germany's state-owned stud farms, the Marbach. Initially, Arab blood was introduced, and later Spanish and Barb *(42)* mares were used along with heavier Friesian *(50)*

stallions. The prototype Württemburg was created by an Anglo-Norman type of cob. However, the greatest development to the breed was made by the introduction of Trakheners, notably a stallion called Julmond in the 1960s, which lent size and scope to the breed. The Württemburg is medium-sized, slightly stocky, but well-proportioned, and is bred with competition in mind. It is long-lived, hardy, and easy to keep.

As a breed it is noted for its good disposition and excellent, true action.

below: The Wielkopolski combines speed and stamina with a natural jumping ability.

Wielkopolski

height *16–16.2 h.h.*
(64.2–66.1 ins; 163–168 cm)
color *all solid colors*
conformation *handsome head; strong neck; powerful body; deep through girth; well-sloped shoulders; strong quarters; strong hock joints; round, open feet*

Originating in Poland, the Wielkopolski is an amalgamation of two older Warmbloods, the Poznan and the Masuren, neither of which now exists. The Poznan was developed around 150 years ago through a mix of Arab *(42)*, Thoroughbred, Hanoverian *(53)*, and, later, Trakehner blood. The Masuren was largely of Trakehner origin. The modern-day Wielkopolski was developed using these two breeds with outcrosses made to Thoroughbreds, Arabs, and Anglo-Arabs *(40)*. It is bred in central and western Poland and is a sound competition horse with plenty of quality. The Wielkopolski is a handsome horse with good paces, displaying an easy walk, straight trot, and ground-covering canter and gallop. Although the heavier examples of the breed can be used for work, the emphasis is on a lighter animal that can perform in competitive disciplines. The Thoroughbred influence has given the breed speed and stamina and it possesses an excellent jumping ability. The Wielkopolski can be ridden or driven.

heavy horses

Ardennais

height 15.3 h.h. (63.4 ins; 161 cm)
color roan
conformation straight profile; medium-length neck; strong shoulders; compact body; deep chest; broad loins; large, strong legs; profuse feathering on lower limbs

Believed to be descended from horses in northeastern France some 2,000 years ago, the Ardennais was developed during the 19th century and belongs to both France and Belgium. By using a variety of outcrosses, the breed was developed into two specific types: a light-draft horse and a powerful work-horse. Arab *(42)*, Thoroughbred *(66)*, Percheron *(72)*, and Boulonnais were used to produce the lighter type, while the bigger type, known as the Ardennes du Nord, derives from outcrosses to the Brabant. This was the old Burgundy horse, the Auxois, which has co-existed with the Ardennais for hundreds of years. The Ardennais's strength and stamina equipped it well for use in military operations, but the modern-day animal was developed specifically for use in agriculture. It is a docile and exceptionally hardy animal, well equipped to cope in harsh

above: *Sometimes described as being built like a tractor, the Ardennais is bred for heavy agricultural work.*

environments. Although it is used mainly for draft work, it is also bred for its meat.

The Comtois originates from the eastern regions of France and is closely related to the Ardennais. It shares the same free action and is used for all types of light draft work.

below: *One of Europe's noblest draft horses, the Boulonnais.*

Boulonnais

height 15.3–16.3 h.h.
(63.4–67.3 ins; 161–171 cm)
color gray
conformation *refined head; thick, arched neck; strong shoulders; prominent withers; broad chest; well-sprung ribs; muscular hindquarters; strong limbs; short, thick cannons; visibly veined skin*

The most elegant of all the heavy horses, because of its strong oriental influence, the Boulonnais is a native of northwest France. The breed can be traced back to Roman times, when oriental horses were introduced into France in the first century A.D. In the 14th century a heavier stamp of animal was developed for use as a warhorse. Thereafter Spanish blood was introduced to increase the breed's soundness and to produce a more active animal. During the 17th century two types of Boulonnais emerged: a lighter, more active version, and a heavier agricultural horse that is still bred today. Two world wars and the rise of mechanization seriously threatened this breed, but it has nevertheless survived. The Boulonnais is used on some farms and is also bred for its meat.

right: *The Brabant has short but extremely strong legs and great hardness of feet.*

Brabant
(Belgium Heavy Draft)

height *16.2–17.2 h.h.*
(66.1–70 ins; 168–178 cm)
color *roan, chestnut*
conformation *plain, relatively small head; short, powerful neck; short, deep and compact body; powerful rounded quarters; short, strong limbs; plentiful feathering*

Horses similar in type to the Brabant, or Flanders Horse, as it was originally known, are believed to have existed since Roman times. The breed is thought to descend directly from the ancient Forest Horse. Between the 11th and 16th centuries warhorses were bred in Flanders and these had a great influence on a number of breeds. The Flanders Horse was the foundation for both the Shire *(72)* and Clydesdale *(70)* breeds and contributed toward the development of the Suffolk Punch *(73)*. Belgium breeders used established bloodlines and a stringent policy of selection to develop a horse that was ideally suited to their country, and subsequent judicious inbreeding has been practiced to preserve the breed's qualities. In the latter part of the 19th century three principal lines were established for the Brabant: the Gros de la Dendre (founded by Orange), which produced massive bay horses; the Gris du Hainaut (founded by Bayard), known for breeding gray, dun, and red-roan horses; and Colosses de la Mehaique (founded by Jean I), which produces exceptionally strong horses with very good limbs.

The Dutch Draft Horse was developed from the Brabant at the beginning of the 20th century by using native mares of Zeeland type and occasional outcrosses to Belgian Ardennais. The breed is particularly large but with a free-moving action and quiet temperament.

Breton

height *15.3–16.3 h.h.*
(63.4–67.3 ins; 161–171 cm)
color *chestnut, roan*
conformation *square head; straight profile; short, strong, arched neck; strong, broad body; powerful quarters; short, strong legs with some feathering; well-shaped feet*

Based on the primitive horse of northwest France, the Breton was originally divided into four distinct types, one of which was a heavy riding horse. Today only two of the types are recognized: the lighter Breton Postier and the Heavy Draft. The latter was developed from outcrosses to Ardennais, Boulonnais, and Percheron *(72)*, while the former had infusions of Boulonnais, Percheron, and some Norfolk Roadster blood. Both types share one stud book and are performance-tested in harness. The Heavy Draft is a large, hardy animal with great strength and stamina. It is still sometimes used for work but is also bred for its meat. The Breton Postier is a lighter weight, active horse, with energetic and free paces. It is used for lightweight draft work and for improving and upgrading poorer stock. The tail is normally docked.

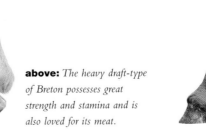

above: *The heavy draft-type of Breton possesses great strength and stamina and is also loved for its meat.*

Clydesdale

height *16.2 h.h. (66.1 ins; 168 cm)*
color *bay, brown, gray, roan*
conformation *straight profile; long neck; well-sloped shoulders; high withers; short back; well-sprung ribs; muscular quarters; straight limbs; profuse fine feathering; good feet*

The Clydesdale originated in the Clyde Valley in Lanarkshire, Scotland and derives from native draft stock crossed with imported Flemish stallions. Later, a significant amount of Shire *(72)* blood was used to such a degree that some believed that the two were part of a single breed. However, by the 19th century a distinctive type had been developed and in 1877 the Clydesdale Horse Society was formed. The breed is noted for its docile temperament and natural elegance that has made it popular worldwide. During the 19th century the Clydesdale was exported in large numbers as far afield as North America and Australia. It is a particularly sound breed with good limbs and feet, equally suited to agricultural or heavy draft work.

below: *The Clydesdale, which has been exported all over the world, has particularly good limbs and feet.*

Italian Heavy Draft

height *15–16 h.h. (60.2–64.2 ins; 153–163 cm)*
color *chestnut, roan*
conformation *relatively fine head tapering to small muzzle; slightly arched neck; well-developed shoulders; deep chest; compact body; deep girth; broad croup; short, strong limbs; boxy feet*

The Italian Heavy Draft was originally developed during the second half of the 19th century as a result of crossing native mares with imported Brabant *(69)* horses from Belgium. There were further outcrosses to Boulonnais *(68)* and Percheron *(72)* to upgrade the stock. These animals were then crossed with the Breton Postier, from which the breed inherited its active paces. The result is a quick-moving, lighter type of draft animal. The modern breed is compact, with a relatively fine head, although it is somewhat coarse of limb. It has a kind and willing nature and energetic paces. As with all heavy breeds, the Italian Heavy Draft has gradually declined in number over the years. Today it is bred as much for its meat as for use on farms.

Jutland

height *15–16 h.h. (60.2–64.2 ins; 153–163 cm)*
color *chestnut, roan*
conformation *heavy, plain head; short, thick neck; broad chest; broad, flat withers; muscular quarters; short limbs; round joints; heavy feathering on lower limbs*

Originating in Denmark, the Jutland (not pictured) is derived from the coldblooded Forest Horse of prehistory. By the 12th century it had developed into a sturdy warhorse, enduring and economical to keep. However, it was not until the 19th century that the modern Jutland began to emerge. The modern breed is a result of outcrosses to the Cleveland Bay *(45)* and Yorkshire Coach horses but it is most influenced by the Suffolk Punch *(73)* (through the stallion Oppenheim LXII, imported to Denmark in 1860), which it closely resembles. The breed is a medium-sized draft horse with a free action. The numbers of Jutlands have steadily declined during the 20th century because of the increase in mechanization. However, these horses can still be seen pulling drays on city streets or in the show ring. Its connection with the Suffolk Punch has resulted in its chestnut coloring, with flaxen mane and tail. Unlike the Suffolk, it has profuse feathering on the lower limbs. The Jutland is a docile and willing worker.

Noriker

height *16–17 h.h. (64.2–68.1 ins; 163–173 cm)*
color *brown, black, chestnut*
conformation *straight profile; medium-length neck; deep girth; compact body; strong limbs; clean joints; ample bone; sound feet*

One of Europe's oldest coldblooded breeds, the Noriker traces back to heavy warhorses developed by the Romans, but it was not recognized as a breed until the mid-16th century, when it was included in the Salzburg Stud Book. The most importance influence on this breed was the introduction of Spanish blood, which added refinement and

left: *The Italian Heavy Draft, while still used agriculturally in northern and central Italy, is now bred more for its meat.*

North Swedish

height *15–15.2 h.h.*
(60.2–62.2 ins; 153–158 cm)
color *any solid color*
conformation *large, squarish head; short neck; sloping shoulders; deep back; rounded quarters; strong limbs*

The North Swedish (not pictured) has its roots in the ancient Scandinavian breeds and is closely related to Døle Gudbrandsdal. However, it was not until the end of the 19th century that a breed society was set up to bring about some uniformity to a breed that had largely relied on a mixture of imported stock.

Strict selective breeding policies are now implemented and the North Swedish is performance-tested in forestry-related tasks. As a result of these breeding policies, the breed is an active, strong horse, known for its easy temperament and longevity.

enhanced its action. The Noriker is a powerfully built workhorse of medium size. It displays good movement and is inherently sound, hardy, and easily managed. The breed is strictly regulated with rigorous inspections and performance tests.

breed. It is, however, suited to all types of light draft work and remains popular in its native land of Normandy. It has retained its energetic action and possesses a particularly active trot.

Norman Cob

height *15.3–16.3 h.h.*
(63.4–67.7 ins; 161–171 cm)
color *chestnut, bay*
conformation *sensible head; strong neck; good shoulders; compact, stocky body; short back; powerful quarters; short limbs; good bone; little or no feathering*

The Norman Cob (not pictured) was developed at the beginning of the 20th century, and descends from the ancient bidets horses that lived before the time of the Roman Empire. The breed originated at the famed French studs of Le Pin and Sainte Lo when a distinction was made between the active cavalry remounts and the heavier light-draft types. The tails of the latter were docked. The Norman Cob gained its name after its British counterpart and became a recognized breed. The Cob is powerful and stocky but lacks the massive proportions of a true heavy draft

below: *Breed standards for the Noriker are strictly adhered to.*

Percheron

height *16–17.2 h.h. (64.2–70 ins; 163–178 cm)*
color *gray, black*
conformation *fine head; long ears; long, arched neck; sloping shoulders; prominent withers; deep girth; sloping hindquarters; massive limbs; good joints; strong feet; minimal feathering*

The Percheron comes from the La Perche region of Normandy in France, probably tracing back to the eighth century. In the 18th century Arab sires were used to upgrade Percheron stock. One of the most important bloodlines was the Percheron stallion Jean le Blanc, foaled in 1830, by the Arab stallion Gallipoly. The strength, soundness, and longevity of the breed has made it particularly suited to a number of roles. Throughout the Percheron's history it has served as a warhorse, carriage horse, and agricultural horse. The Percheron is capable of adapting to different climates—a characteristic inherited from its Eastern ancestors— and is therefore in great demand in other countries. The breed can be used under saddle, and displays surprisingly free-moving paces for its size.

Russian Heavy Draft

height *14.2–14.3 h.h.*
(58.25–59.4 ins; 148–151 cm)
color *roan, chestnut*
conformation *attractive, light head; strong frame; wide chest; short clean legs; approximately 8.7 ins (22 cm) of bone; medium-sized feet; minimal feathering on lower limbs*

Developed in the early 1900s, the Russian Heavy Draft was bred at the Khrenov and Derkul state stud farms in the Ukraine, initially using Ardennes stallions on native mares. There were subsequent crosses with a variety of other breeds, including the Brabant *(69)* and some Percherons. Orlovs *(61)* were later introduced to give increased activity to the breed. After a general decline in numbers, a breeding program was initiated in the 1920s, with the aim of producing a willing horse with active paces suitable for general agricultural

work. Originally known as the Russian Ardennes, the breed was only registered as the Russian Heavy Draft in the 1950s. Built along similar lines to a heavy Cob, the breed has a strong frame, is early-maturing—reaching almost full size before it is two years old—and long-lived.

Shire

height *16.2–17.2 h.h.*
(66.1–70 ins; 168–178 cm)
color *black, gray, bay*
conformation *Roman nose (convex profile); kindly eyes; long neck; short, muscular back; deep girth; hard limbs with 11–12 ins (28–30 cm) of bone; profuse, fine, silky feathering on lower limbs.*

The Shire derives from an old warhorse known as the English Black. Native stock was crossed with imported Flanders and Friesian *(50)* horses to produce first a warhorse, then a general draft animal. The breed takes its name from the English midland shires of Leicestershire, Lincolnshire, Derbyshire, and Staffordshire, and was first used in 1884. At the same time, the Old English Cart Horse Society was changed to the Shire Horse Society.

A good temperament coupled with strength, stamina, and soundness made it immensely popular and it was exported to countries all over the world, including North and South America, Russia, and Australia. This versatile breed was used for all kinds of heavy agricultural and draft work. As with other breeds, the spread of mechanization during the 20th century led to a decline in numbers. However, there has been renewed interest in the breed, especially since the 1960s, and the Shire is now a popular feature at shows and can be seen pulling beer drays in cities.

Suffolk Punch

height *16–16.3 h.h.*
(64.2–67.3 ins; 163–171 cm)
color *chesnut*
conformation *large head; straight or convex profile; deep neck; low shoulders; massive, rounded quarters; deep, rounded body; short, strong legs; little feathering; relatively small, sound feet*

The Suffolk Punch takes its name from the English county in which it was traditionally bred, and is the oldest and purest of the British heavy breeds. Developed in the 16th century, the Suffolk was probably influenced by the Norfolk Roadster and the Flanders Horse. The latter added weight, strength, and the distinctive chestnut coloring, and the former lent activity and hardiness to the breed. All Suffolks trace back to one sire, Thomas Crisp's Horse of Ufford, foaled in 1768. The breed color is always chesnut (this spelling is peculiar to the breed), and the term "punch" aptly describes this short-legged, heavy-bodied horse. The lack of feathering on the lower limbs made it ideally suited to working the heavy clay soils of East Anglia and its equable temperament, soundness, and longevity made it a popular agricultural and draft animal. Despite the effect of mechanization, the breed is a popular sight in the show ring and is still used to plow and pull drays.

Vladimir Heavy Draft

height *16.1 h.h. (64.4 ins; 163.5 cm)*
color *usually bay*
conformation *large, somewhat long head; long muscular neck; deep through the girth; broad back; long limbs; some have heavy feathering on the lower limbs*

The Vladimir (not pictured) was only recognized as a breed in 1946 and its type and character were finally fixed in 1950. The breed was originally developed at Russian State Studs, where native mares were crossed with both Clydesdales and Shires. Other breeds such as Suffolk Punch and Percheron were used to a lesser extent.

The Vladimir is an extremely powerfully built heavy horse suitable for both agricultural and draft work. It is naturally docile but displays particularly active paces, bearing in mind its size, and matures early.

top: *Oldest and purest of the British heavy breeds, the Suffolk Punch is still bred in the county it was named after.*

left: *In Britain the name "Shire" is almost synonymous with draft horses and the breed has found new popularity in the show ring.*

above: *New Forest Ponies.*

right: *A Dülmen mare and foal.*

Ponies are indigenous to many parts of the world and are renowned for their surefootedness, hardiness, and their instinct for self-preservation. Each breed has evolved characteristics to meet the demands of its environment.

principal pony
breeds

breed is versatile—a popular choice in harness, both in the show ring and in harness racing. It is also a useful children's pony.

Australian Pony

height *12–14 h.h. (48.4–56.3 ins; 123–143 cm)*
color *all solid colors*
conformation *refined head showing Welsh Mountain influence; widely spaced eyes; excellent forelegs and shoulders; curved neck; well-formed back; good hind legs*

The Australian Pony has evolved from a number of breeds and types imported to Australia by early settlers. The strongest influence, however, is that of the Welsh Mountain Pony that the overall outline of the Australian Pony strongly resembles. The breed has had other infusions of Shetland,

American Shetland

height *up to 10.5 h.h. (42 ins; 107 cm)*
color *any color*
conformation *long head; straight profile; sloping shoulders; strong loins; short body; long, slim limbs*

The American Shetland bears little resemblance to its British counterpart. It's the result of crossing purebred Shetlands with Hackney ponies *(85),* with some Arab *(42)* and Thoroughbred *(66)* infusions. The breed, which is one of the most popular in North America, was established during the 1880s and the American Shetland Pony Club was formed at the latter end of that decade. With its high, exaggerated trot, the American Shetland resembles a small Hackney Pony. This good-natured

Hackney, Thoroughbred, and Arab blood. The Australian Pony has a long, smooth stride, is compact and strong, and has correct conformation. The set and slope of the shoulders result in a stride that is very comfortable for the rider, and this makes the breed a popular choice of mount for children and small adults. The Australian Pony Stud Book Society was formed in 1929.

Avelignese

height *13.2–14.2 h.h.*
(54.3–58.25 ins; 138–148 cm)
color *chestnut, flaxen mane and tail*
conformation *neat head; short, heavy neck; broad back; low withers; short legs; good feet; minimal feathering on lower leg*

A heavier version of Austria's Haflinger, the Avelignese comes from the mountainous regions of central and northern Italy. While essentially a coldblood, the breed shares common ancestry with the Haflinger in the Arab foundation sire El Bedavi. This is most notable in its face, which shows distinct Arab influences. The Avelignese is docile, hardy, and surefooted, and is known for its longevity. It is bred selectively in a number of Italian regions, including Tuscany and Bolzano, and is mainly used for light agricultural work and as a pack animal.

Bashkir

height *14 h.h. (56.3 ins; 143 cm)*
color *chestnut, bay*
conformation *coarse head; short neck; heavy, somewhat straight shoulders; short limbs; flat back; hard feet*

Originating in the southern foothills of the Urals in Bashkiria, the breed evolved centuries ago but was only recognized in the 19th century, when breeding centers were developed to improve the stock. The Bashkir is an important commodity in the region and

is used not only as a pack animal and in harness, but also for riding. It is used for its meat and milk—Bashkir mares can produce more than 300 gallons of milk during a seven-month lactation period. Generally kept in herds, the breed is incredibly hardy, and has been known to survive in temperatures as low as -40°C. The Bashkir has now developed into two distinct types: the mountain type, which is used under saddle, and the heavier steppe type, which is mainly used in harness. One of the distinguishing features of this breed is its thick, curly coat.

top right: *As well as being ridden, the Bashkir is bred for its meat and milk.*

right: *The Italian Avelignese is particularly long-lived and combines a docile temperament with a hardy nature.*

Basuto

height *14.2 h.h. (58.25 ins; 148 cm)*
color *bay, brown, chestnut, gray*
conformation *quality head; long neck; upright shoulders; long back; hard feet*

The Basuto (not pictured) is not an indigenous breed to Basutoland, but evolved from Arab and Barb *(42)* stock imported to South Africa from Java during the 17th century. Interbreeding with local stock has resulted in what is now known as the Basuto Pony. The breed is thick-set and has exceptional powers of endurance. It is tough, hardy, and capable of carrying considerable weight. The Basuto is a versatile breed and is used not only as a pack animal but also for riding, polo, and racing.

right: *The Caspian Pony—believed to be descended from an Asian desert horse.*

Batak

height *13 h.h. (52.4 ins; 133 cm)*
color *all colors*
conformation *long, narrow back; high rump; slim legs, lacking bone; high-set tail; hard feet*

The Batak has been bred selectively on the island of Sumatra since the time of the Dutch colonists. Since then, Arab stallions *(42)* have been used to improve and upgrade the breed. The Batak is an integral part of island life and is used as a working animal, for riding, and for

left: *Eastern influence has given the Batak Pony its spirit and agility.*

upgrading poor stock on neighboring islands. Arab influence has given the pony an attractive appearance with good proportions. The breed is docile, but retains its eastern spirit and agility. As with other Indonesian breeds, the Batak is easy to manage. It is able to exist on limited rations and is therefore economical to keep.

Caspian

height *10–12 h.h. (40.6–48.4 ins; 103–123 cm)*
color *bay, chestnut*
conformation *short, fine head; short ears; long, arched neck; sloping shoulders; narrow but deep body; slim limbs with dense bone; hard, strong feet*

The Caspian Pony is believed to be descended from Horse type 4 (prototype Arab)—a primitive desert horse from western Asia. It has different physical characteristics from other equines, including an extra molar on each side of the upper jaw, a different shaped scapula, and a different formation of the parietal bones of the head. Despite its ancient origins, the breed was "discovered" in the 1960s in a remote mountainous region of northern Iran, not far from the Caspian Sea. Since then, careful breeding programs have been set up and the Caspian is now bred in Europe, Australia, New Zealand, and America. Despite its diminutive size, this hardy breed is fast and enduring and possesses an excellent jumping ability. Although termed a pony, the Caspian resembles a miniature horse.

Chincoteague

height *12 h.h. (48.4 ins; 123 cm)*
color *all colors*
conformation *weak forehand; short, compact body; poorly developed joints; weak hind legs*

The Chincoteague Pony inhabits the islands of Chincoteague and Assateague, off the coast of Virginia. It is most likely derived from stock abandoned or strayed from Spanish colonists in the 17th century. In the early part of this century, the Chincoteague Fire Department—which is responsible for the management of the islands—became interested in this breed. They used Welsh *(92)* and Shetland *(91)* blood, together with Pinto, to upgrade island stock that was showing signs of degeneration, including stunted growth and conformational defects, such as misshapen limbs and narrow chests. Each year the ponies are rounded up on the uninhabited island of Assateague and made to swim over to Chincoteague, where the young stock are sold off. The Chincoteague has some popularity as a children's riding pony.

below: *The Chincoteague is native of islands off the coast of Virginia, and is popular as a children's mount.*

Connemara

height *up to 14.2 h.h. (58.25 ins; 148 cm)*
color *mainly gray but also brown, dun, black*
conformation *fine, neat head; long neck; well-sloped shoulders; deep body; well-developed quarters; strong, sound feet*

The only indigenous equine of Ireland, the Connemara is a sturdy, general-purpose riding pony that, when crossed with a Thoroughbred, produces a larger, all-around riding horse. Originating on the western coast of Ireland, the breed is one of the best performance ponies in existence and is now bred throughout the world. The Connemara is descended from the Irish Hobby of the 16th and 17th centuries. Over the years a variety of breeds, including Arab *(42)*, Welsh Cob *(92)*, Thoroughbred *(66)*, and Clydesdale *(70)*, were imported to improve the native stock. The Connemara Pony Breed Society was founded in 1923 and the English Connemara Society in 1947. The Connemara is a quality pony, capable of excelling in most equestrian disciplines but retaining hardiness and common sense.

right: *A popular choice as a family pony, the Dales is sound, active, and surefooted.*

Dales

height *14.2 h.h. (58.25 ins; 148 cm)*
color *black, dark brown, occasionally gray*
conformation *neat head; strong shoulders; short, powerful limbs; strong quarters; hard feet; feathering on heel*

One of the heaviest of Britain's native breeds, the Dales Pony comes from the eastern Pennine Hills in Northumberland, Durham, and Yorkshire. It is believed to be descended from horses of Roman times, when the ancient Friesian breed was introduced to

northern Britain. Other blood used includes Norfolk Roadster, Welsh Cob *(92)*, and Clydesdale *(70)*. The breed is closely related to its near neighbor, the Fell, which originated on the western side of the Pennines. The Dales Pony is renowned for its stamina and sensible temperament. It is sound, active, and surefooted, and makes an ideal riding and driving pony. It is quite capable of carrying an adult, and is a popular choice as a family pony.

Dartmoor

height *up to 12.2 h.h. (50.4 ins; 128 cm)*
color *bay, brown*
conformation *small, neat head; strong neck; fine, sloping shoulders; muscular hindquarters; high-set tail; excellent limbs; hard feet*

Originating in the Dartmoor area of Devon, in southwestern England, the breed has inhabited the moorlands for thousands of years. Its habitat close to the south coast of Britain means that it has been subjected to a greater degree of outside influence than its neighbor, the Exmoor. The breed has been infused with Arab *(42)*, Welsh, and

below: *A popular children's pony, the Dartmoor is sensible and surefooted with an equable disposition.*

Thoroughbred blood but probably the greatest modern influence was that of The Leat, foaled in 1918 by the Arab Dwarka out of a Dartmoor mare.

A decline in numbers of Dartmoor ponies after the Second World War led to the setting up of the Dartmoor Pony Society Scheme, which encourages farmers to register purebred ponies and to provide them with the services of pedigree stallions. The aim of the scheme is to establish a pool of pure-bred ponies that breeders can use to retain the true native characteristics. The Dartmoor makes an ideal first pony. It is narrow in build, sensible, and surefooted, with a long, low action and an equable temperament.

right: *The Dülmen is one of only two native breeds in Germany and exists in a semi-wild state.*

Dülmen

height *12.2 h.h. (50.4 ins; 128 cm)*
color *brown, black, dun*
conformation *shortish neck; upright shoulders; short back; weak hindquarters*

One of only two pony breeds native to Germany—the second of which, the Senner, is now considered to be extinct—the Dülmen is a breed of mixed origins. It now exists in a semi-wild state on the estate of the Duke of Croy in the Meerfelder Bruch, Westphalia. Despite their current lack of importance, it is believed that both these German pony breeds may have had some influence on the development of the early Hanoverian horse *(53)*.

above: *Probably one of the oldest equine breeds in the world, the Exmoor is an excellent all-around performance pony.*

below: *A miniature horse, rather than a pony, the Falabella is generally kept as a pet.*

Exmoor

height *12–12.3 h.h.*
(48.4–51.2 ins; 123–130 cm)
color *bay, brown, dun; no white markings*
conformation *wide forehead; prominent "toad" eyes (heavy-lidded); wide nostrils; strong body; short limbs with good bone; "ice" tail; neat, hard feet*

Britain's oldest native breed, and possibly one of the oldest equine breeds in the world, the Exmoor is currently on the Rare Breeds Survivals Trust's critical list. There are currently only three principal herds left on Exmoor, and the breed tends to lose type when bred away from its natural habitat. The Exmoor shares some similarities with the ancient Celtic pony, in that it has a distinct jaw formation and the beginnings of a seventh molar, features that do not occur in other equines. Other features of this breed are the hooded "toad" eyes and the "ice" tail, so called because it has a short, thick growth of hair at the top. Exmoor's isolated position in west Somerset and north Devon means that in its natural habitat the breed has had little outside influence of other blood. The Exmoor has the strength to carry a grown man. It is intelligent but, if not handled correctly, can be willful. It makes an excellent all-around performance pony for an older child, but will, if well schooled and handled, make a suitable mount for a small child.

Falabella

height *up to 7.5 h.h. (30 ins; 59 cm)*
color *all colors*
conformation *large head in proportion to size; flat withers; straight shoulders; weak hind legs; limbs may lack bone; low-set tail*

The Falabella was developed in Argentina by crossing the smallest Shetland ponies *(91)* with very small Thoroughbreds *(66)*, then by crossing the smallest animals thereafter. The object was to produce a near-perfect equine specimen in miniature. Unfortunately, inbreeding has, at times, resulted in some weakness of conformation, although the

best examples of the breed retain the qualities of good Shetland ponies. The breed, known as a miniature horse rather than a pony, is mainly kept as a pet, although the animals can be used in harness. They are not suitable for riding. Many of the breed have attractively spotted coats.

Fell

height *up to 14 h.h. (56.3 ins; 143 cm)*
color *Black, brown, bay, gray*
conformation *well set-on head; strong neck; good, sloping shoulders; deep, compact body; strong hindquarters; well-formed feet with blue horn*

The Fell, like its neighbor and close relation, the Dales *(80)*, was influenced by the Friesian *(50)* and the now extinct Scottish Galloway—a swift, surefooted pony with great stamina. Although lighter than the Dales Pony, the Fell is still enormously strong; it was used during the 18th century as a pack pony for transporting lead and coal. Official distinction between the Fell and Dales ponies did not come into being until 1916, when the Dales Pony Improvement Society and the Fell Pony Society were formed. The Fell displays particularly good paces, including a fast walk and a lively trot, and makes a good, all-around riding pony. Surefooted and agile across country, the Fell excels at trekking. It is a popular driving pony, too, equally suited to being ridden or put in harness.

Fjord

height *13–14 h.h. (52.4–56.3 ins; 133–143 cm)*
color *shades of dun; black, dorsal eel strip; silver mane and tail with black hairs in center*
conformation *broad forehead; small pony ears; muscular neck; powerful body; strong limbs; flat joints; hard, sound feet*

Norway's famous Fjord Pony closely resembles the Przewalski's Horse *(62)*, from which it is descended, with its pronounced dorsal eel stripe and zebra markings on the legs. Believed to have inhabited Norway since prehistoric times, this breed is perfectly adapted to the mountainous regions of its birthplace. The Fjord is inherently surefooted and has great stamina.

A hardy and sound pony, it is ridden, driven, and also used as a pack pony. A distinctive feature of the breed is its silvery colored mane that is, by an ancient tradition, clipped so that the black hairs at the center stand out above the rest.

top: *Good paces are a feature of the Fell Pony, which is surefooted and agile.*

left: *Descended from Przewalski's Horse, the Fjord is perfectly adapted to its mountainous homeland.*

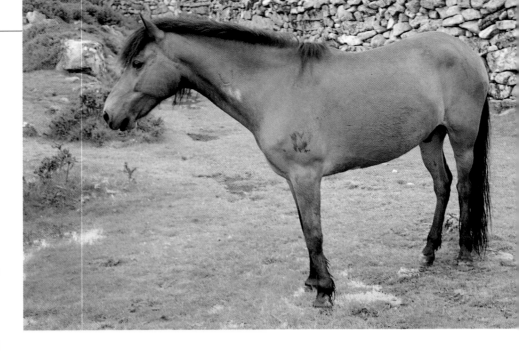

Galiceno

height 14 h.h. (56.3 ins; 143 cm)
color all solid colors
conformation fine head; lightlybuilt frame; compact
body; long back; upright shoulders; sound limbs

Originating from Galicia in Spain, the
modern Galiceno of Mexico has
inherited the running walk for which
horses from Galicia were famed. The
breed derives from early Spanish horses
and has inherited a hardy constitution
from the Sorraia (91) and Garrano
breeds of the Iberian peninsula. The
Galiceno is intelligent and versatile and
has natural agility and speed, which
make it a popular choice for ranch
work. It is also used in harness and as a
means of everyday transport. The
Galiceno was recognized as a breed in
the late 1950s, and is a popular choice
of mount for older children.

below: *Agility and intelligence make the
Galiceno a natural ranch worker.*

Garrano (Minho)

height up to 12 h.h. (48.4 ins; 123 cm)
color dark chestnut
conformation small, pretty head; shortish,
strong legs; compact body

Closely related to the Sorraia, the
Garrano or Minho Pony originates in
the fertile mountain valleys of the
Garrano do Minho and the Traz dos
Montes in Portugal. While there is no
doubting its ancient ancestry,

above: *A popular children's pony, the Garrano has
inherited its physical characteristics from the Arab.*

this breed has been greatly influenced
by infusions of Arab (42) blood that
have left it more refined than its close
relation. The Garrano is a quality pony

right: *The natural high-stepping action of the Hackney Pony is most often seen in the show ring.*

with a pretty head and notably good conformation. It is both hardy and sure-footed. As a result, the breed is used for hauling timber and as a pack horse, but it is also in demand as a riding pony.

Gotland

height *12–12.2 h.h.*
(48.4–50.4 ins; 123–128 cm)
color *brown, dun, black, chestnut, gray, palomino*
conformation *small head; strong neck; lightly built frame; poor hind legs; low-set tail*

The most ancient of all Scandinavian breeds, the Gotland or Skogruss Pony is believed to be a descendant of the primitive Tarpan, although infusions of Arab blood were introduced during the 19th century. The breed once lived in a semi-wild state on the island of Gotland and in the forest of Lojsta; now the ponies are selectively bred on the Swedish mainland and in other Scandinavian countries. Originally used mainly on farms, the Gotland is now more frequently used as a riding pony and has a fast walk and trot and a good jump. The breed is hardy and easily managed.

Hackney Pony

height *12.2–14 h.h.*
(50.4–56.3 ins; 128–143 cm)
color *all solid colors*
conformation *characteristic pony head; high neck carriage; compact body; depth through chest; symmetrical quarters; strong hocks; clearly defined joints*

This breed has all the pony characteristics but shares the stud book with the Hackney Horse (52) and, to a large extent, has a common ancestry in the Norfolk and Yorkshire Trotters. The Hackney was largely the creation of Cumbrian breeder Christopher Wilson (northwest England), who in the 1880s created a distinctive type based on the Fell Pony (83) with Welsh outcrosses. The breed's hardy constitution is the result of being left to fend for itself throughout the winter on the fells (moors). The Hackney possesses courage and stamina, and has a natural high-stepping action. It is now largely confined to the show ring, where its spectacular movement is displayed to best effect.

left: *Believed to have descended from the primitive Tarpan, the Gotland is the most ancient of all Scandinavian breeds.*

Haflinger

height *14.2 h.h. (58.25 ins; 148 cm)*
color *chestnut with flaxen mane and tail*
conformation *large eyes; wide nostrils; well-formed muscular neck; long body; deep girth; strong limbs; good feet*

A hardy mountain pony originating in the Austrian Tyrol, the Haflinger can be traced back to the Arabian on one side—its foundation sire is El Bedavi XXII—and the coldblooded heavier types on the other—its base is the now extinct Alpine Heavy Horse. This combination makes it particularly suitable for both draft work and riding. Its mountain homeland has contributed to the hardiness of this breed and young stock are still traditionally raised on the Alpine pastures. The Haflinger is small, but powerfully built and surefooted, with a long-striding, particularly free action inherited from its Eastern forbears. It is known for its placid and docile temperament. The Haflinger is also long-lived—some members of the breed remain fit and active until the age of 40 years.

Highland

height *13–14.2 h.h. (52.4–58.25 ins; 133–148 cm)*
color *gray, various shades of dun, bay, black*
conformation *wide forehead; wide nostrils; strong neck; compact body; well-sprung ribs; strong back, usually marked with a dorsal eel stripe; hard, dark hooves; silky feathering on legs*

The Highland is one of the heaviest of Britain's native breeds and is a native of the Scottish highlands and the Western Isles. It is a breed of great antiquity—ponies of this type have inhabited these regions since the Ice Age. There were originally two types of Highland: the more substantial mainland type standing up to 14.2 hands high, and the somewhat lighter Western Isles type. However, the Highland Pony Society, founded in 1923, no longer recognizes these two distinctions. The modern Highland breed is a result of various outcrosses, including Percheron *(72)*, Clydesdale, *(70)* and Arab *(42)*, the former adding size and weight, the latter improving quality and movement. The Highland is surefooted and strong, capable of carrying shot deer down from the hills. Hardy and docile, it is a popular all-around riding pony. When crossed with a Thoroughbred, the Highland makes a useful hunter.

Hucul

height *12–13 h.h (48.4–52.4 ins; 123–133 cm)*
color *dun, bay, piebald*
conformation *medium-sized head; upright shoulders; short body; flat withers; strong limbs; uniformly sound feet*

Native to the Carparthian mountain region of Poland, the Hucul is believed to be descended from the primitive Tarpan; more recently, Eastern influences have been introduced to improve its quality. For hundreds of years, the Hucul performed the duties of a pack

below: *Hardy and docile, the Highland is a popular all-around riding pony.*

below: *Selective breeding has improved some of the Hucul's conformational defects.*

below: *Having lived in the region since the 9th century, the Icelandic horse has a special place in the history of the country.*

animal, carrying heavy loads over difficult mountain terrain, often in extreme weather conditions. The modern pony has been bred selectively, which has helped to improve some points of conformation, such as the structure of the hind leg. The Hucul is most often used in harness but continues to be a useful pack pony, combining strength and endurance with a docile temperament.

Icelandic

height *12.2–13.2 h.h.*
(50.4–54.3 ins; 128–138 cm)
color *any color*
conformation *heavy head; powerful frame; short neck; compact body; strong hindquarters; strong limbs*

The Icelandic Horse—known as a horse despite its small size—is one of the purest of all breeds; it has had no infusions of outside blood for nearly a thousand years. Horses were taken to Iceland during the 9th century and thus have a special place in the history of the country. The breed is incredibly tough and able to withstand the severe weather conditions of the region. In the late 1870s selective breeding of the ponies was introduced to the horse-breeding area of Skagafjordur. The breed has five gaits (paces): walk, trot, gallop, skied (pacing), and tölt (a running walk). The Icelandic Horse is intelligent and docile, and has great powers of stamina and endurance. It is used for work and for riding.

above: *Despite its small stature, the Java has the strength to pull the Javanese version of a taxi—the two-wheeled* Sados.

Java
height *12.2 h.h. (50.4 ins; 128 cm)*
color *all colors*
conformation *neat head; weak neck; weak hindquarters; long back; cow-hocked*

Native of the island of Java in Indonesia, this breed has been upgraded by Arab and Barb *(42)* blood. Unlike some of the other Indonesian breeds, the Java has little of the Arab look, although it has inherited considerable stamina from the breed. The influence of the Barb has contributed to its strength and toughness. Despite its small stature, it is mainly used to pull the two-wheeled Javanese sados that are used as taxis on the island; it is also ridden. The Java is willing and easily managed.

Konik
height *13 h.h. (52.4 ins; 133 cm)*
color *shades of dun*
conformation *short neck; compact back; fairly upright shoulders; well-made hind legs; well-muscled quarters; deep girthed*

The breed is largely the base for the reconstructed primitive horse, the Tarpan, which is kept in maintained herds in Popielno. The Konik is widespread throughout Poland and is descended from the primitive Tarpan, from which it retains characteristics such as hardiness and a robust constitution. The Konik is widely used for working the land—its upright

above: *A number of breeds have influenced the New Forest Pony, which is renowned worldwide for its free movement and excellent temperament.*

shoulders and low withers make it eminently suitable for harness work. It is bred in Polish state studs at Jezewice and Popielno. The breed has a kindly temperament, is easily managed, and is able to survive on limited rations. Many ponies have the mouse-dun color and black dorsal stripe typical of the Tarpan.

New Forest
height *up to 14.2 h.h. (58.25 ins; 148 cm)*
color *all solid colors*
conformation *large head; shortish neck; long, sloping shoulders; strong hindquarters; well-shaped limbs; good feet*

The accessibility of its natural habitat in the south of England means that the New Forest has mixed origins with influence from a number of breeds. In the 18th century the Thoroughbred stallion Marske, sire of Eclipse, one of the greatest racehorses of all time, was used on New Forest mares. A century

left: *The Konik is the base for the reconstructed Tarpan, which is kept in herds in Poland.*

later, an Arab stallion belonging to Queen Victoria roamed with the herd. Other breeds, including Welsh Mountain *(92)*, Dartmoor *(80)*, Highland *(86)*, Fell *(83)*, Dale *(80)*, and Exmoor *(82)*, were later used to preserve the true pony substance. Many New Forest ponies are now stud-bred, but the New Forest still supports a number of ponies whose owners carry out an annual round-up to select stock for sale. Hardy, surefooted, possessing notably free movement, and with an excellent temperament, the New Forest is an ideal choice for a family pony. The breed is popular throughout the world.

Peneia

height *10–14 h.h. (40.6–56.3 ins; 103–143 cm)*
color *any solid color*
conformation *somewhat coarse head; narrow body; pronounced withers; slender legs*

Bred in the Eleia region of Peloponnese, Greece, the Peneia is connected to the Pindos Pony and is used as a pack animal and for light farmwork, and is also ridden and driven.

The breed varies considerably in height; the larger examples tend to be those resulting from more judicious breeding strategies. It is a strong, sturdy animal, capable of surviving on minimal rations.

Pindos

height *13 h.h. (52.4 ins; 133 cm)*
color *bay, black, brown*
conformation *longish head; long, narrow back; pronounced withers; small joints; hard feet*

The Pindos Pony (not pictured), also known as the Thessalonian, originates in the Thessaly and Epirus regions of Greece. It is thought to be a direct descendant of the Thessalonian, with infusions of the ancient Peloponnese, Arcadian, and Epidaurian blood. This tough and hardy breed can survive on minimal forage and is remarkably sure-

right: *Versatility is the main strength of the Greek Peneia Pony.*

right: *A versatile children's mount, the Pony of the Americas was recognized as a breed in the 1950s.*

footed. Its feet are very hard and rarely have to be shod. The Pindos is very versatile, but it has a reputation for being rather stubborn. It is used for farm work and as a pack pony, and is suitable for riding and driving. Pindos mares are used to mate with donkey stallions for breeding mules.

Pony of the Americas

height *11.2–13.2 h.h. (46.5–54.3 ins; 118–138 cm)*
color *Appaloosa markings*
conformation *neat head; slightly arched neck; sloping shoulders; short back and loins; well-made legs; wide, sound feet*

The Pony of the Americas is an officially recognized breed. The Pony of the Americas Club was formed in 1956 by the instigator of the breed, Lesley Boomhower, whose aim was to produce a versatile children's mount. The foundation of this breed was the stallion Black Hand—by a Shetland stallion out of an Appaloosa mare—with later outcrosses to Arabs and Quarter Horses. The breed has substance and refinement, with a straight, free action that makes it a popular all-around riding pony. It is equally suited to being ridden in Western or English saddle or put to a harness.

above: *The Sable Island Pony is a hardy breed that displays some conformational defects.*

Sable Island Pony

height *14–15 h.h. (56.3–60.2 ins; 143–153 cm)*
color *all solid colors*
conformation *large head; narrow frame; withers underdeveloped; weak quarters; low-set tail*

Along with the Chincoteague *(79)*, the Sable Island Pony is one of the last few "wild" equine populations. The breed is thought to have been introduced to Sable Island off Nova Scotia, Canada, in the early 18th century. It is believed to have Norman origins and to have derived from French stock. A tough, hardy breed, it existed on poor vegetation on this largely barren island. Its conformation is only moderate, with a head that is out of proportion to its somewhat narrow body. It is generally docile and can be easily managed if trained while relatively young.

Sandalwood

height *13 h.h. (52.4 ins; 133 cm)*
color *all colors*
conformation *small, fine head; wide chest; deep girth; hard joints; tough feet*

Originally from the Indonesian islands of Sumba and Sumbawa, the Sandalwood has been greatly influenced by infusions of eastern blood. These have resulted in its distinct Arab characteristics of a small, fine head with large eyes. Named after the islands' main export, these ponies have been a popular export commodity themselves, mainly to Australia, where they are in demand as children's ponies. The breed is fast and active, excelling at the

above: *While being the smallest, the Shetland is also one of the strongest of Britain's native breeds.*

Indonesian sport of bareback racing. The Sandalwood has exceptionally hard feet that do not have to be shod.

Shetland

height *not exceeding 10.5 h.h. (42 ins; 107 cm) at four years and over*
color *all colors except spotted*
conformation *small, well-carried head; small, erect ears; broad muzzle; large nostrils; full mane and tail; short, strong limbs; deep body with short back; tough hooves with blue horn*

The smallest of Britain's native breeds, the Shetland is also one of the strongest. Originating from the Shetland Isles some 100 miles (160 km) north of Scotland, the Shetland is descended from ponies that lived in that habitat as long as 10,000 years ago. In the past it was used as a pack pony by crofters to collect peat and work the land. Its strength also made it eminently suitable for use as a pit pony in coal mines on the Scottish mainland. The Shetland is inherently hardy, having adapted to the islands' harsh environment. It is long–

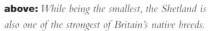

left: *The Sandlewood has been greatly influenced by infusions of Eastern blood.*

above: *Small in stature, the Skyrian is always referred to as a horse by its breeders.*

from the Asiatic Wild Horse and the Tarpan. Small of stature, with a relatively large head and dun coloring, it bears a distinct likeness to the Tarpan. The eel stripe and zebra markings on the legs are another indication of its links with the primitive equine types. In its native land the breed has traditionally been used as a mount for local cowboys and for light agricultural work. The modern Sorraia is an attractive pony that is resistant to both heat and cold and is capable of existing on very poor quality vegetation.

above: *Portugal's Sorraia has an attractive appearance and is tough and enduring.*

lived and sound and is bred extensively outside the islands. It is intelligent, if somewhat strong-willed, and is a popular choice as a children's riding pony. The breed has active paces that make it an ideal driving pony.

Skyrian

height *11 h.h. (44.5 ins; 113 cm)*
color *bay, dun*
conformation *neat head; compact, narrow body; upright shoulders; narrow croup*

Despite its diminutive size, up to 11 hands high, this breed is referred to as the Skyrian Horse by its breeders. Originating on the island of Skyros in the Aegean Sea, the Skyrian has horse-like proportions that may indicate a connection to the old Thessalonian Horse. A dorsal eel stripe and zebra markings on the lower limbs indicate links with primitive equines. Although Skyros has been a home to ponies since ancient times, little is known about the origins of this breed. It is mainly used as a pack animal on its native island. However, a good-natured temperament coupled with stamina and an ability to jump make it useful as a child's mount.

Sorraia

height *12.2–13 h.h.*
(50.4–52.4 ins; 128–133 cm)
color *mainly gray-dun*
conformation *black-tipped, high-set ears; powerful, short neck; compact body; low-set tail; good length of rein*

The Sorraia's homeland is in Portugal, between the rivers Sor and Raia. The breed is believed to have descended

Sumba/Sumbawa

height *12.2 h.h. (50.4 ins; 128 cm)*
color *dun with dorsal stripe*
conformation *common head; short neck; strong back*

The Sumba and Sumbawa ponies are identical, showing a distinctly primitive appearance. They originate from the two Indonesian islands from which they take their name, although their ancestry can be traced back to the wild Mongolian Horse. The Sumba and Sumbawa are fast, agile, and willing; they are also exceptionally hardy and,

despite their small size, can easily carry grown men. They are used as pack animals and in the Indonesian national sport of lancethrowing. The breed's coloring is primitive—essentially dun with a black dorsal stripe, dark mane and tail, and black or zebra markings on the lower legs.

below: *Primitive markings indicate the Sumba/Sumbawa's ancient origins.*

Timor

height *12 h.h. (48.4 ins; 123 cm)*
color *black, bay, brown*
conformation *common head; short neck; full mane and tail; straight-backed; upright shoulders; high-set tail*

The Indonesian island of Timor, off the northern coast of Australia, supports a proportionally large number of Timor ponies. They exist on the relatively good grazing available on the savannas. The breed originates from ponies introduced to the island in the 16th and 17th centuries by the Portuguese, and later by Dutch colonists. The latter are likely to have encouraged the use of ponies as a means of transport. Since the beginning of the 19th century, the Timor has been exported to Australia, where it is popular as a child's mount. The breed is strong, agile, and sure-footed, and displays a high level of common sense.

Welsh Mountain (Section A)

height *12 h.h. (48.4 ins; 123 cm)*
color *all solid colors*
conformation *small, neat head, tapering to muzzle; small, pointed ears; long, sloping shoulders; strong back; deep girth; strong limbs; well-shaped feet*

The Welsh Mountain Pony (section A in the Welsh Pony and Cob Society Stud Book) is the base from which the Welsh Pony and the two divisions of Welsh Cobs have developed. Indigenous ponies have inhabited the Welsh hills from as long ago as Roman times, and Thoroughbred *(66)*, Arab *(42)*, Hackney *(52)*, and Barb *(42)* blood have all had an influence on this breed. The patriarch of the Welsh Mountain, Dyoll Starlight, foaled in 1894, is believed to have had Arab blood traced back through his dam. And, since the beginning of the 20th century, the appearance of the modern-day Welsh Mountain Pony has been sustained and is a direct result of careful selection within the breed. The Welsh Mountain is recognized as one of the most beautiful of all the native breeds, with its fine, slightly dished face and wide-spaced eyes. It is courageous, hardy, spirited; and kindly, making it an ideal choice for a children's mount. It is also used for carriage driving.

below: *Courageous and spirited, the Welsh Mountain Pony is the base of the Welsh breeds.*

above: *A popular competition pony, the Welsh Pony (section B) displays long, low action.*

Welsh Pony (Section B)

height *13.2 h.h. (54.3 ins; 138 cm)*
color *all solid colors*
conformation *small, neat head; good, sloping riding shoulders; well-muscled quarters; strong, hard legs; flat joints; deep girth; hard feet*

The Welsh Pony is derived from the Welsh Mountain Pony and small Welsh Cobs, with Arab, Barb; and Thoroughbred influences. The foundation of the modern breed is attributed to Tan-y-Bwlch Berwyn, foaled in 1924 by the stallion Sahara. A son of that stallion, Berwynfa, founded the famous Coed Coch herd. Larger than the Welsh Mountain, the best examples of the Welsh Pony retain true pony characteristics. It makes a popular all-around competition pony, performing well both under saddle and in harness. The Welsh Pony combines long, low action with courage and intelligence.

Welsh Pony of Cob Type (Section C)

height *13.2 h.h. (54.3 ins; 138 cm)*
color *all solid colors*
conformation *thick-set neck, carried high; well-laid-back shoulders; deep girth; powerful quarters; compact outline; strong limbs; small amount of feathering on the heels*

The Welsh Pony of Cob type (section C) is the smaller of the two Welsh cobs. It originated as a farm and general work pony and was extensively used in slate mines at the beginning of the

20th century. After the Second World War, the type declined in numbers and a new type, designated section C in the stud book, was opened in an attempt to preserve this workmanlike pony. Originally the cob type developed from a cross of Welsh Mountain mare and small cob stallion, but later on the most important of section C stallions had strong Welsh Mountain connections. Today, many examples of the breed are a result of mating stock registered as section C in the stud book. The Welsh section C is a larger, sturdier version of the Welsh Mountain, tough and sound, with good limbs and feet. It makes a popular all-around riding pony, hardy and economical to keep, and capable of taking part in all types of equestrian activities.

Welsh Cob (Section D)

height *no smaller than 14.2 h.h. (58.25 ins; 148 cm)*
color *all solid colors*
conformation *neat head; small, pony ears; strong, arched neck; compact body; well-sprung ribs; short, powerful limbs; large, flat joints; extraordinary flexion in hock joints to give superb action*

The Welsh Cob (section D) derives from the Welsh Mountain Pony, with subsequent outcrosses to Norfolk Roadsters and Yorkshire Coach Horses in the 18th and 19th centuries. The cob is the largest of the Welsh breeds and, uniquely for British native ponies, has no upper height limit for showing purposes. Tough, courageous, and spirited, the breed is famed for its spectacular trotting ability—largely a result of its Norfolk Roadster ancestry. Traditionally used for heavy work on hill farms, the breed is now more often used under saddle or in harness. A cross with the Thoroughbred *(66)* is the basis for the Welsh part-bred that has increased in popularity over the years and produces an excellent competition horse. Economical to keep, the Welsh Cob is hardy, robust, and inherently sound.

top: *Spectacular trotting ability is a feature of the hardy Welsh Cob (section D).*

left: *The workmanlike Welsh Pony of Cob Type (section C) is used in all types of equestrian activities.*

The shape, size, nature, and colors of horses have all been determined by evolutionary factors, but man has placed his own stamp on the modern equine. Whatever the influence, natural or human, the diversity of horses is very much a part of their beauty and a source of their fascination.

types and colors

types of horse

Cob

height *up to 15.3 h.h. (63.4 ins; 161 cm)*
color *any color*
conformation *intelligent head; short, strong neck; sloping shoulders; short, strong body; deep girth; powerful hindquarters; strong limbs with plenty of bone; sound feet*

The cob is a sound, mannerly horse with a marked weight-carrying ability. It makes a popular all-around mount. The cob goes well in harness and has a willing and even temperament. The best cobs often have strong Thoroughbred/Irish Draft influence, but heavy horses are also used. The cob combines strength and endurance with a kind and sensible nature. In addition to its strength, a cob's ability to gallop and jump makes it an ideal mount for hunting. The cob is also seen in the show ring where it is shown with a hogged mane to emphasize its strong neck. Cobs are shown in two weight classes: lightweight (capable of carrying up to 196 lbs [88.9 kg]) and heavyweight (capable of carrying over 196 lbs).

Hack

height *14.2–15.3 h.h. (58.25–64.4 ins; 148–161 cm)*
color *any solid color*
conformation *neat, quality head; elegant neck; well-sloped shoulders; compact body; well-developed hindquarters; fine, graceful limbs, with ample bone below the knee; good, neat feet*

The term "hack" dates back to the days when wealthy people rode "pack" hacks in London's fashionable parks. There was also a "covert" hack, a horse used by hunting folk to ride to the meet; once there, they would transfer to their waiting hunter. Today's show hack is similar to the former type. It is generally Thoroughbred, although it can be part-bred, and is an attractive, elegant, and well-mannered mount. The hack combines excellent conformation with good riding shoulders and elegant limbs. It must, however, have at least 8 inches (20.3 cm) of bone below the knee. In the show ring the hack must display faultless manners and correct training. Hacks are divided into two height classes: large (15–15.3 h.h./60.2–63.4 ins; 153–161 cm) and small (14.2–15.h.h./58.25–60.2 ins; 148–153 cm).

Hunter

height *14.2 h.h. (58.25 ins; 148 cm) upward*
color *any*
conformation *well set-on, quality head; honest eye; sloping shoulders; compact body; deep girth; well-sprung ribs; powerful hindquarters; strong limbs; ample bone; excellent feet*

A hunter is used for riding to hounds and is bred with speed, endurance, and boldness in mind. Hunters vary in

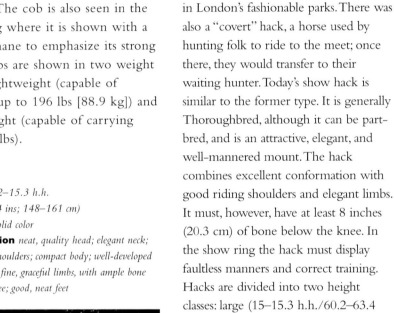

left: *The cob is cherished for its intelligence and generally handsome appearance, and characterized by its all-around usefulness.*

left: *The hack must combine excellent conformation with good riding shoulders and elegant limbs.*

Riding pony

height *12–14.2 h.h. (48.4–58.25 ins; 123–148 cm)*
color *all solid colors*
conformation *refined head; well-spaced eyes; small muzzle; long, elegant neck; well-sloped shoulders; medium-length back; deep girth; well-muscled quarters; well-formed feet*

The riding pony combines the elegant proportions of a Thoroughbred with pony looks and character. It evolved through a mixture of native pony blood (mainly Welsh section A and B), Thoroughbred, and Arab. The art of riding pony breeding is to combine the presence and free action of the Thoroughbred with the good sense and substance of the native pony. In essence, the riding pony is a children's version of the show hack. In the show ring ponies are divided into three height classes: up to 12.2 h.h. (50.4 ins; 128 cm); up to 13.2 h.h. (54.3 ins; 138 cm); and up to 14.2 h.h. (58.25 ins; 148 cm).

type, depending on the hunting country in which they are used. In England and Ireland, hunting is an age-old sport, and these countries have traditionally produced the best hunters. A Thoroughbred/Irish Draft cross is often used, but many good hunters have some native pony blood. A hunter should have excellent conformation and plenty of stamina and speed. It must give a good, comfortable ride, and display natural jumping ability. Hunters are prominent in the show ring in England and Ireland. They are divided into three weight-carrying categories: lightweight (capable of carrying up to 175 lbs; 79.4 kg); middleweight (capable of carrying between 175 and 196 lbs; 79.4 and 88.9 kg); and heavyweight (capable of carrying over 196 lbs). There are also ladies' hunters (ridden side-saddle); small hunters (between 14.2–15.2 h.h./58.25–62.2 ins; 148–158 cm); and working hunters, which are required to jump a small course.

Polo pony

height *15.1 h.h. (61.4 ins; 156 cm)*
color *any*
conformation *refined head; long, well-muscled neck; prominent withers; short back; well-sprung ribs; straight limbs; short cannons; good, sound feet*

Polo ponies are fast, agile, and supremely balanced. The game of polo was originally introduced to Europe and the Americas by the British, who had played the game in India. The first polo ponies were generally based on British native mares crossed with small Thoroughbreds. Today the majority of polo ponies have strong Argentinian connections—this country has dominated the sport for many years. These ponies are generally based on imported Thoroughbreds crossed with part-bred Criollo stock. The resulting stock is put back to Thoroughbreds to increase the speed. The height of the polo pony was originally fixed at 14.1 h.h. (57.5 ins; 146 cm), but this was abandoned after the First World War. Today the average height is around 15.1 h.h. (61.4 ins; 156 cm).

below: *The riding pony has the proportions of a Thoroughbred combined with the characteristics of a pony.*

colors and markings

markings

On the face
star—white marking between/above the eyes

snip—small white marking on the muzzle

stripe—vertical white mark down the center of the face

blaze—wide white mark down the nose

On the legs
sock—white mark extending just below the knee to the foot

stocking—white mark extending up over the knee

ermine—white mark around the coronet

zebra—dark rings of hair on the lower limbs (these marks have primitive origins)

hooves
dark horn, pale horn, mixed horn

The color of a horse's coat is determined by the animal's individual genes, of which there are 39. Many coat colors are developed through selective breeding, but some—gray, bay, brown, and black—are dominant. Chestnut is recessive, meaning that both parents have to be chestnut for the offspring to be that color.

colors

gray the definition of gray is a black skin with a mixture of white and black hairs. The color range varies from almost white to very dark, known as iron gray. Other variations include flea-bitten (dark specks) and dappled (rings of dark hair on a gray coat).

bay a red-brown coat with a black mane, tail, and lower limbs. The color variation includes red (bright bay) and yellowish (light bay) hairs.

brown a mixture of black and brown hairs with black mane, tail, and limbs.

black black coat, mane, tail, and limbs.

chestnut reddish-brown coat with a similar colored mane, tail and limbs. The color varies from pale golden to very dark chestnut (liver).

dun black skin with yellowish hairs. Black mane and tail. Dun animals often have a black dorsal eel stripe. Coat colors vary from yellowish to mouse, while blue dun has grayish/black hairs.

strawberry roan white hairs on a chestnut/brown body, giving the coat a slightly pink tinge. Variations include white hairs on a black/brown body, known as blue roan.

palomino golden coat with a much paler, often white, mane and tail.

skewbald large areas of brown and white.

piebald large areas of black and white.

sports and recreation

From the elegance of dressage to the thrill of the rodeo, the modern horse plays an important part in sport and leisure.

above: *The thrill and spectacle of flat racing is encapsulated at the Kentucky Derby.*

left: *Of the basic elements in modern three-day eventing, the eventing section is a whirl of drama and excitement as horses and riders compete against the clock.*

dressage

The origins of dressage date back to the fourth or fifth century B.C. Grecian friezes show horses and riders performing the equivalent of modern dressage movements. And a book by the Greek statesman, Xenophon, suggests that the art of riding was developed to a high degree at this time. Hundreds of years later, dressage became more widely practiced as a means for training horses going into battle. Horses that could turn quickly and leap sideways, and that could be ridden and controlled with one hand, were a desirable asset on the battlefield.

In the late seventeenth century, dressage began to develop in a way we would recognize today. Schools of equitation began to evolve, most notably the Spanish Riding School in Vienna. In France, a famous military school, the Cadre Noir, developed into a school of classical equitation when the need for warhorses diminished after the Second World War.

The natural desire of humans to compete meant that dressage inevitably developed into a sport. The first dressage competition was held in 1873, and the first international competition in 1902. A decade later, dressage was included as an Olympic sport.

All riders can benefit from basic dressage training. The word itself—taken from the French verb *dresser* (to train)—does not simply mean the art of performing difficult and impressive maneuvers. Dressage involves training a horse to improve its natural balance and movement.

European domination

In Britain, a country in which racing and hunting flourish, dressage was slow to establish itself as a sport. On the continent, where the sports of racing and hunting are less common, the lack of open land combined with a harsh winter climate meant that indoor riding quickly became very popular. Europeans therefore have a considerable advantage in the progress of dressage training.

Some breeds or types of horse are better suited to dressage than others. In Europe, there was early specialization in the breeding of sport horses with suitable athletic paces and, most importantly, accommodating

Carl Hester is one of a growing band of riders who are contributing to Britain's success on the international stage.

temperaments. The British Thoroughbred's sensitive nature and highly developed instinct for flight make this horse generally unsuitable for the strict discipline of dressage, but it has been used to modify the dressage horse since the 1970s.

Since the 1930s, the acceptance of dressage as a sport in Britain has slowly grown. Dressage has also flourished worldwide. It has benefited from an increase in horse ownership, the sport's economy on space, the rising number of indoor and all-weather outdoor arenas, and the realization that dressage improves all horses in all equestrian disciplines.

Dressage competitions are held throughout the year. Britain now hosts international competitions and boasts an ever-increasing number of riders able to compete at the Grand Prix level. In 1993 Britain achieved its highest team result when it came in third in the European championship at Lipica.

In the early years of the sport, Sweden and Russia were top international competitors. More recently, Germany has dominated dressage championships around the world. With its rigorous training system, Germany produces large numbers of riders able to compete at the highest levels. Despite having fewer riders, the Netherlands is closing the gap on Germany. In the United States, the use of imported specialist horses and continental trainers means that this country is fast becoming an international force to be reckoned with.

Evidence of the sport's worldwide growth could be seen at the 1998 world championships in which 19 teams and 84 individual riders took part, the highest number ever.

below: *Germany's Nicole Uphoft and Rembrandt, who scored team and individual gold medals at both the 1988 and 1992 Olympics.*

competition dressage

Dressage is divided into different levels. Within each level there are tests to assess the standard of training achieved. Many riders never rise above the level of novice, but even a horse that is trained to novice level will be a better ride than one that has not been trained at all.

Individual countries follow their own training regimes. They have set tests to assess the progress of training at different levels. However, all advanced tests are ridden in an arena that is 180 by 60 feet (60 by 20 m) and international competitions are governed by the Fédération Equestre Internationale (FEI), which sets the tests and the rules.

Advanced dressage is divided into two levels. The first, "Small Tour," includes the Prix St. Georges test and the Intermediaire I. The second, "Big Tour," includes the Intermediaire II and the Grand Prix.

The ultimate dressage test, the Grand Prix is of seven minutes' duration. It includes the *haute ecole* "Airs" of *passage* and *piaffe*, in which the horse must show 12–15 steps on each occasion, together with 15 consecutive one-time changes, and canter and walk pirouettes. The paces within, and the transitions to and from different paces, are also marked.

left: *Jennie Loriston-Clarke competing in the 1988 Olympics. Tests are broken down into individual movements, with each one being marked out of 10.*

It takes a horse at least five years to learn the Grand Prix movements and an animal will only be established at this level at about the age of 12. With careful training, a horse is capable of competing at the Grand Prix level until the age of 17. Younger, precocious horses are able to learn the movements, but training and performing can put great strain on young joints and muscles. This, combined with the mental pressure, can shorten the working lives of competition horses.

dressage judging

Competition dressage is marked by trained and assessed judges. As it is not an exact science and very much a matter of subjective choice, the marking of dressage competitions can be controversial. Five judges are therefore usually recommended at international competition, with one to three judges for national contests.

Each test is broken down into individual movements, and each movement is given marks out of 10.

Marks are also given for the quality of the paces, degree of athleticism, willingness to perform, and the effect of the rider. A preliminary test carries a maximum score of 200, and a Grand Prix of 500. Final scores are usually expressed as percentages. The highest winning scores are usually between 70 and 75 percent.

freestyle dressage

A specialist pursuit, dressage has never enjoyed the mass spectator appeal of other equestrian disciplines. However, dressage to music—known as freestyle competition or kür—has recently found favor and become a more spectator-friendly sport. Riders create their own tests based around compulsory movements. These are ridden to a musical score of a pre-determined length. The best freestyle competitors use music that is chosen to reflect the type of horse they are riding and its style of movement. Since 1995, all dressage championships have taken the kür into consideration. The scores of the

above: *Perfect timing is imperative in the "pas de deux."*

Grand Prix, the Grand Prix Special, and the kür are added together to determine the overall champion. Given the range of tests the performers are required to undergo, it is remarkable that gold and silver medalists can finish less than 1 percent apart. Team competitions are decided on the results of the Grand Prix alone. The best three scores from each team are added together to determine the winners.

Although the training ideals for dressage are still set by the standards of the Spanish Riding School, very few people now study and perform "classical" dressage. Nevertheless, displays by the world-famous gray Lipizzaner stallions are a treat, not just for dressage enthusiasts, but for anyone who appreciates the finer aspects of the ultimate training of the horse.

eventing

At the beginning of the twenty-first century, nearly 100 years after the sport was first introduced, eventing is one of the fastest-growing equestrian disciplines. About 150 horse trials take place in Britain each year, with more than 45,000 runners—a number that grows annually. The sport's governing body, the British Horse Trials Association, has almost 8,000 members. Eventing combines the three disciplines of dressage, cross-country, and show jumping, and is the most complete test of a horse's abilities.

the early days

Eventing began as a trial for military riders in France—to this day it is still referred to as the "Military" on the continent. In 1902 a competition was held in Paris exclusively for military chargers and officers. It was the first

above: *The testing speed and endurance phase of the three-day event includes the roads and tracks section.*

contest to resemble the modern sport of horse trials. It consisted of four phases: dressage, endurance—involving a 2.5-mile (4-km) steeplechase and a 31-mile (50-km) long-distance ride—and show jumping. The competition proved so popular that it became an annual event. In 1922 certain changes were made—the long-distance ride was shortened and a cross-country test was introduced—and the competition became more like the three-day event we know today.

the three-day event

The competitors in the three-day event complete three different tests—dressage, speed and endurance, and show jumping—held over three consecutive days. Dressage requires

left: *Blythe Tait who, along with Mark Todd, has led New Zealand's domination of the sport on the international stage.*

competitors to perform a test of medium difficulty, comprising about 17 different movements. The test is marked by a panel of three judges who award a total of 250 marks. Marks are awarded for each movement, and there are also points for paces, impulsion, submission, and seat of the rider.

Speed and endurance, the second test, is divided into four phases, A to D. Phases A and C are held over roads and tracks totaling a distance of 6 to 12 miles (10–20 km) to be ridden at a trot or slow canter. Phase B is a steeplechase, ridden at a gallop over a course of 1 to 2.5 miles (2–4 km), including between 18 and 12 fences.

The most important phase of this test is D, the cross-country phase, which is 3 to 5 miles (5–8 km) long and includes up to 32 fixed obstacles. The cross-country phase is ridden at a gallop. Competitors incur penalties

for falls (of either horse or rider, or both), refusals, crossing tracks, and exceeding the time limit allowed for each phase.

The final section, show jumping, comprises a course of up to 12 fences. Penalties are incurred for knocking down fences, refusals, falls, and exceeding the maximum time allowed. All horses must undergo veterinary checks before the start of each test, and must pass each one before the competitor is allowed to continue. The same horse-and-rider combination must complete all three sections. In a team competition there are three or four members. The best three final scores go toward the final placing of the team, and the fourth is discarded.

Olympic history

The inclusion of a three-day event in the 1912 Olympic Games in Stockholm, Sweden, and at the 1920 Games in Antwerp, Belgium, greatly increased the sport's popularity. However, it was not until the Paris Games in 1924 that the sport adopted its modern format, albeit with a much more complicated scoring system (it also included phase E, a "run-in" section after the cross-country test, which has long since disappeared).

Of the ten teams competing at Paris in 1924, Holland won both team and individual gold medals; their champion rider, Lt. Adolph van der Voort van Zyp, won by 122.5 points, a margin that would be unheard of today, particularly since scoring procedures have been overhauled and the system of bonus points dropped. At the 1928 Games in Amsterdam, both titles again went to Holland. Their gold medal victor, Lt. C.P. Mortanges, went on to win again at the 1932 Olympics in Los Angeles.

Britain captured its first Olympic medal—a team bronze—at the 1936 Berlin Games, but was eliminated on home ground at the 1948 London Olympics, where the United States won the team gold. Britain's abysmal performance in 1948 prompted the

Tenth Duke of Beaufort to hold a national three-day event on his Badminton estate in order to improve the standard. The horse trials at Badminton have since become the most celebrated occasion in the eventing calendar—many competitors covet an award here even more than an Olympic medal.

The 1956 Stockholm Olympics marked the dawn of a golden era for British eventing. British teams won gold medals there and then in Mexico (1968) and Munich (1972). At the Munich Games, Richard Meade became the first—and so far the only—British rider to capture an individual gold.

In the 1964 Tokyo Olympics, women were allowed to compete for the first time. The sole female competitor, Lana Dupont of the United States, finished 33rd with Mr. Wister and won a team silver medal. However, it would be another two decades before women stood on the rostrum to receive individual Olympic medals. At the 1984 Games in Los Angeles, Karen Stives of the United States took the silver and Britain's Ginny Holgate (now Elliot) won the bronze. The United States also won the team gold.

antipodean domination

The 1984 Los Angeles Olympics were special for another reason. They marked the beginning of antipodean

domination of the Olympic Games, and of other top eventing competitions. New Zealand's Mark Todd claimed the individual gold astride the great Charisma, an achievement they both repeated in Seoul four years later.

When Mark Todd first arrived in Britain in 1978, few people had heard of him, but he has since become one of the most famous and, arguably, the greatest event riders of all time. He has won three times at Badminton, three times at Burghley (the only other top "four star" three-day event in Britain besides Badminton), and has gained an "open European" title, a European Championship open to competitors from countries outside Europe.

Another New Zealander, Blythe Tait, claimed the individual title at the Olympic Games in Atlanta, Georgia, in 1996. Here a radical overhaul of the format by the International Olympic Committee saw the team and individual competition divided into two separate classes for the first time. Riders were prohibited from representing their country on the same horse in both classes, a decision unpopular with competitors that is nevertheless likely to remain in force. Australia has also enjoyed its fair share of success, with Matt Ryan winning both the individual and team golds at the 1992 Barcelona Games.

European and world championships

Although the European Championship was "opened" to the rest of the world in 1995 and 1997, since its inception in 1953 it has otherwise been reserved solely for riders from European nations. The Championship takes place every two years, and Britain has won team golds 15 times. Major Laurence Rook and Major Frank Weldon (later director and course designer at Badminton) got the ball rolling for future British success by claiming the individual gold and silver medals, respectively at the first Europeans, held at Badminton, and HRH Princess Anne, who did much to increase the popularity of eventing during her top-level career, won the Championship in 1971 with Doublet.

The World Championship was started in 1966 at Burghley, and Britain has won five team gold medals since then. The first Championship was beset by difficulties because of an outbreak of African horse sickness, which led to a ban on the transport of horses from Europe. The statutory minimum of five teams entered the competition, the United States, Ireland, and the Soviet Union flying in their horses direct from

home. Two riders have won the World Championship twice: Bruce Davidson of the United States (in 1974 and 1978) and Blythe Tait (in 1990 and 1998). Ginny Elliot won the title in Gawler, Australia, in 1986, and went on to win the alternative competition staged in the northern hemisphere (for those unable to afford the expense of transporting horses to Australia) at Bialy Bor, Poland.

levels of competition

While few riders possess the talent or even the ambition to represent their country at the Olympic, World, or European Championship levels, there are other three-day events where they can compete. In 1974 and 1988, respectively, two "three-star" three-day events were set up at Bramham and Blenheim in Britain, and there are others scattered around the globe. Britain hosts four "two-star" competitions for intermediate-level horses—Windsor, Burgie, Blair Castle, and Weston Park—and two "one-stars" for the most inexperienced horses at Sansaw Park and Tweseldown (site of the 1948 Olympic cross-country test).

To qualify for a three-day event, horses must have completed several one-day competitions. There are 150 of these to choose from in Britain, far more than in any other country in the world, and this is why so many riders from the southern hemisphere have relocated to the United Kingdom.

As the name implies, all phases take place on the same day at a one-day event. They take place in a different order than at a three-day event— dressage is followed by show jumping and cross-country. There are no roads, tracks, or steeplechase courses to contend with, no veterinary inspections, and there are different classes to suit varying levels of experience. The grades run from pre-novice and novice to intermediate and advanced, and competitors progress through the levels when they gain points for a placing. One-day events were originally established to provide preparation for Badminton, but they have since become a nationwide network of competitions in their own right.

developments in the sport

The most recent developments in eventing include an increased number of CIC competitions. These are international one-day events that offer substantial prize money. CIC competitions are popular with riders because large sums can be won without the necessity of subjecting horses to the rigors of a three-day event.

Another major change has been to alter the scoring system for three-day events in an attempt to simplify the sport for spectators and the media. Dressage scores are now given in whole numbers (without decimal points, as used to be the case) and more emphasis is placed on the cross-country test, with penalties doubled for a refusal and a fall.

Change is always problematic in the sporting world, but even the experts acknowledge that the many disciplines of eventing make it a complicated sport for the uninitiated. However, there is little to equal the thrill of seeing great horses and riders speeding around a cross-country track, and the popularity of eventing with competitors and spectators remains undiminished.

above: *Burghley horse trials, which hosted the first World Championship in 1966.*

left: *Ginny Elliot, holder of one world and three European gold medals.*

show jumping

The sport of show jumping has developed into the most professional of the three main equestrian disciplines outside of racing. With major shows around the world throughout the year and huge sums in prize money, show jumping's most successful riders are millionaires. While in Britain the heyday of its popularity with the general public appears to have passed, in Europe and the United States riders are still household names and companies are as eager as ever to engage in lucrative sponsorship deals.

the early years

Its growth is relatively recent—earliest records of organized show jumping competitions date back to the 1860s. Ireland, home of steeplechasing, was one of the early hosts of major competition. The 1865 Royal Dublin Show offered riders the chance to take "high and wide leaps." France and Russia followed suit, but it wasn't until shortly after the turn of the century that the sport became truly international. At the 1900 Olympic Games held in Paris, three jumping competitions were included: long-jumping, high-jumping, and prize-jumping. Competitions between

Germany and Italy followed, and in 1907 the first International Horse Show was held at Olympia in London.

By the 1912 Stockholm Olympics, eight countries—Belgium, Chile, France, Germany, Great Britain, Norway, Russia, and Sweden—entered a total of 31 competitors and show jumping had come of age. Individual glory went to France's Captain Cariou, with Sweden taking the team gold medal.

By the start of the First World War, Germany had its own Olympic Equestrian Committee, while the United States was quick to follow,

establishing the American Horse Shows Association in 1917. Britain proceeded more slowly, establishing the British Show-jumping Association in 1923 and joining the Fédération Equestre Internationale (FEI) two years later.

Horses attended their first non-European Olympic Games in Los Angeles in 1932, where show jumping attracted 34 competitors. German

below: *Show jumping competitions first began in the 1860s and it has become the most professional of the three main disciplines, with the exception of racing.*

left: *Franke Sloothak is one of a number of talented riders who have contributed to Germany's success on the international circuit.*

dominance of the sport was demonstrated at the following games, held in Berlin, where the host nation swept the board with gold medals in individual and team events in show jumping, dressage, and three-day eventing.

New stars came to the fore at the first post-war Olympics, held in London in 1948, with the team gold medal going to Mexico, Spain collecting silver, and Britain gaining its first Olympic medal, a bronze. The sport was growing rapidly.

In 1948 a junior championship for riders between the ages of 14 and 18 was introduced. The first men's world championship was held in Paris in 1953 and was won by Spain's Francisco Goyoaga. His successor was Hans Gunter Winkler of Germany, whose mare, Halla, also took Olympic gold in Stockholm in 1956. Winkler achieved the feat of collecting a further three Olympic team gold medals at Tokyo, Rome, and Munich.

world and European contests

Two contests have emerged around which the international calendar is organized—the World Championship and the European Championship. World Championships are held every four years. The qualifying rounds produce four leading riders for the final round, in which they ride each other's horses. The simpler European competition, held every two years, involves three initial rounds, with cumulative points deciding the championship.

The first European Championship for women, held in 1957, catapulted one of show jumping's greatest names onto the world stage. Pat Smythe had been the first woman rider to compete at the Olympics in 1956, and at her

first European Championship began a run of success with Flanagan that was to bring them three European titles.

The men's and women's European Championships were amalgamated in 1975 when finally all equestrian competitions were opened to men and women, bringing them into line with the Olympics.

the international stage

The true internationalism of the sport has been shown in the past two decades by the success of a number of different countries. But if any one country currently has the edge, it is Germany, which took both team and individual (Ulrich Kirchhoff) gold medals at the 1996 Atlanta Olympic

Games. The wealth of talented riders, including Ludger Beerbaum, Franke Sloothak, and Kirchhoff, has given Germany a consistent record to build on that of predecessors, such as Gert Wiltfang and Paul and Alwin Schockemohle. In addition to its Olympic glory, Germany boasts the current European and World

Champion, crowned in Rome in 1998.

Holland made its mark in the early 1990s, taking team gold at the Barcelona Olympics and claiming European silver at Mannheim in 1997. For France, team gold medalists at the Montreal Olympics in 1976, the campaign has continued, although top honors have been

elusive, despite the consistency of leading riders such as Michel Robert and Eric Navet.

The United States enjoyed a surge of success on the world stage in the 1980s, taking the 1984 Olympic title on home ground in Los Angeles and cheering on riders such as Greg Best; who took team silver four years later

in Seoul. Best ended the decade with a successful world title bid at Stockholm in 1990.

Britain, with leading riders including the brothers John and Michael Whitaker, Nick Skelton, and Geoff Billington, has not enjoyed Olympic gold medal success in recent years but has always been one of the countries to beat, collecting team silver at the Los Angeles Olympics and a string of European medals, including team gold at St. Gallen (1987) and Rotterdam (1989). Many believe that Olympic success could be key to a rise in popularity in the United Kingdom, where show jumping has lost out to sports such as billiards and golf as a spectator and television event since the heyday of heroes like David Broome and Harvey Smith.

rules

Early show-jumping competitions were, by modern standards, scarcely spectator events. Most of the obstacles looked the same and there was no time limit, so rounds lacked the excitement of a battle against both the elements and the clock.

The rules were confusing. Merely touching a fence incurred penalty points, as did landing within certain demarcation lines around spread fences. Gradually, pressure from competitors forced changes and the evolution of a simple, spectator-, rider-, and horse-friendly system governed internationally under the auspices of the Fédération Equestre Internationale (FEI), which was established in 1921 to bring uniformity to the sport of show jumping.

Courses must generally be completed within a certain time, otherwise time penalties are incurred. Knocking a fence down—either by

left: *Ludger Beerbaum of Germany competing on Ratina at the 1996 Olympics, which saw Germany win both team and individual gold medals.*

dislodging a top pole or demolishing the whole obstacle—incurs four faults. A first refusal, which includes circling in front of a fence, incurs three faults. Six faults are amassed for a second refusal, and elimination is the result of a third. A fall also incurs penalty points.

Competitors are allowed to walk the course first, which enables them to measure the distances between fences, size up any combination fences (those within 39.4 ft/12 m of each other) and figure out the optimum number of strides between each. The course walk can also reveal where corners can be cut and which fences can be tackled at an angle, although there is no substitute for drawing a position late in the order of competitors, so you can watch the class progress and spot any bogey fences. Combination fences, either doubles or triples, often cause problems; negotiating the short distance between the fences is often trickier than clearing the fences themselves.

There are five types of fences: upright, parallels, pyramids, staircase, and water. Course builders use a combination of these to test the ability of horse and rider. Water jumps can be crucial to the outcome of a competition, particularly if the horse is young, inexperienced, or frightened of water.

A crowd-pleaser, although not suited to many horses, the *puissance* competition is a specialized class centering on one particularly high jump. A short course leads up to the high jump, usually a wall, whose height is steadily raised until none but the winner can jump it.

training

Training at home, both over jumps in an arena and over natural obstacles, begins slowly and takes time and patience. Young horses start by trotting over poles laid out on the ground, before progressing to trotting over cavaletti and jumping small fences about 2 feet (60 cm) high.

Once these are negotiated confidently, a variety of colored poles and different obstacles are set up, offering a range of challenges that will keep a young horse interested. Jumping training is interspersed with work on the flat, as well as gentle work across open country, taking in any natural obstacles such as fallen logs, streams, and ditches.

After completing small courses at home and building up to fences of around 3.25 feet (1 m), progress is tested by introducing the horse to small shows, initially not to compete, but to be a spectator taking in the sights and sounds of new activity.

While today the Warmblood is preeminent, traditionally no single breed held the edge. Chief prerequisites for success at jumping have been natural athleticism and enthusiasm, as well as boldness and quick-witted intelligence.

below: *Ireland's Edward Doyle competing on Wingates King Koal at the Royal Windsor Horse Show, England.*

horse racing

Although men have ridden horses in races since time immemorial, it was only after King Charles II was restored to the English throne in 1660 that organized racing took place on a regular basis. Charles II spent part of the year at Newmarket, founding its spring and fall meetings, still pivotal fixtures on the British racing calendar. Queen Anne instituted the Royal Ascot meeting in 1711, and racing first took place on the Knavesmire course at York in 1731. In those days most horses did not race until five years of age, rarely running less than two miles

and frequently as much as four. Matches were popular so larger fields of competitors ran in heats until the first to win twice was the outright winner. The first great racehorse was the second Duke of Devonshire's unbeaten Flying Childers, though he won just two matches at Newmarket as a six-year-old in 1721.

the Jockey Club

The Jockey Club, composed of peers and other wealthy men, was formed in about 1752, when the word "jockey" still denoted either an owner or rider

of horses. At first a social association, the Jockey Club soon assumed control of the racing at Newmarket, later extending its authority to every course in England.

Horses were usually ridden by their owners or stablehands, until Sam Chifney emerged as the first important professional jockey by introducing elements of tactical riding. He was retained by the Prince of Wales for the huge sum of 200 guineas in 1790. The following year Chifney's riding of the Prince's Escape at Newmarket came under grave suspicion, and his downfall

was brought about by Sir Charles Bunbury, the first dominant member of the Jockey Club.

the classics

While Sir Charles Bunbury was Dictator of the Turf between 1768 and 1821, younger, lighter horses began to run over shorter distances and more frequently in single heats like the classics, the five championship races for three-year-olds: The St. Leger, run over a mile and six furlongs (2.8 km) at Doncaster, the Oaks (fillies only, 1 m 4 f/2.4 km, Epsom) in 1779, the Derby (1 m 4 f, Epsom) in 1780, the 2000 Guineas (1 m/1.6 km Newmarket) in 1809, and the 1000 Guineas (fillies only, 1 m, Newmarket) in 1814. As racing of two-year-olds became more widespread, the six-furlong (1.2-km) July Stakes at Newmarket, the oldest juvenile event in the world, was introduced in 1786.

handicaps

The first bookmaker, a man called Ogden who offered odds for every runner, first operated around 1790. One of the first handicaps, in which weights were adjusted to give the

runners theoretically equal chances, was the Oatland Stakes at Ascot in 1791. Popular handicaps introduced later included the Wokingham Stakes, first run over six furlongs at Ascot in 1813, the Chester Cup (2 m/3.2 km Chester, 1824), Northumberland Plate (2 m, Newcastle, 1833), Royal Hunt Cup (1m/1.6 km, Ascot, 1843),

Stewards Cup (6 f/1.2 km, Goodwood, 1840) Ebor (1 m 6 f/2.8 km, York, 1843), Portland (6 f, Doncaster, 1855), Cambridgeshire (1 m 1 f/1.8 km, Newmarket, 1839), and Cesarewitch (2 m 2 f/3.6 km, Newmarket, 1839).

the emergence of National Hunt racing

While the handicaps were becoming popular on the flat, hunting men were organizing their own races across country. The first recorded steeplechases took place in Leicestershire in 1792. The inaugural Grand National was won by the aptly named Lottery in 1839, and the National Hunt Committee was formed for the regulation of racing over fences and hurdles in 1866.

The second Dictator of the Turf was Lord George Bentinck, who held sway between 1832 and 1834. He exposed Running Rein, first in the infamous Derby of 1844, as a four-year-old (rather than three) and introduced many reforms, including starting by flag instead of on the order "go."

Although matches were going out of vogue, one of the greatest of them all took place at York in 1851, when

right: *First staged in 1839, the Grand National remains one of the toughest challenges for National Hunt horses.*

Flying Dutchman, winner of the Derby in 1849, beat the 1850 Derby winner Voltigeur by a length, the weights having been decided by Admiral Rous, the third and last of the great Dictators.

In 1853, West Australian displayed the versatility of the ideal racehorse by becoming the first to complete the Triple Crown by winning the 2000 Guineas, the Derby, and the St. Leger. West Australian was trained at Malton by John Scott, one of the fast-emerging public trainers who ran their own stables instead of being privately employed by rich men. Other trainers of this time included Mat Dawson, a Scotsman who had the Heath House Stables at Newmarket, and his older brother Tom, the first trainer to dispense with "sweating"—galloping heavy, rugged horses long distances to eliminate surplus flesh.

above: *Early morning exercising in Lambourne, Berkshire.*

the American Triple Crown

The United States was soon to have its own Triple Crown, as the Belmont Stakes was established at Belmont Park, New York, in 1867. Six years later the inaugural Preakness Stakes was run at Pimlico, headquarters of the Maryland Jockey Club, older than the Republic

itself. Finally the Kentucky Derby, the "Run for the Roses" since Ben Brush was awarded a garland in 1896, was first staged in 1875. Famous winners of the American Triple Crown include War Admiral (1937), Whirlaway (1941), Citation (1948), Secretariat (1973), and Seattle Slew in 1977.

the French Classics

Although France stages the world's most prestigious international flat race, the Prix de L'Arc de Triomphe, which was first held at Longchamp in 1920, the country was comparatively late in establishing organized racing. The French Jockey Club was established in 1833 by the Duc d'Orleans and Lord Henry Seymour, who later led a breakaway group to form the Société d'Encouragement pour l'Amelioration des Races de Chevaux en France. In 1836 the Prix du Jockey Club, equivalent to the English Derby, was run on a new course established at Chantilly, near Paris, and within a decade France had its other classic races: the Poule d'Essai des Pouliches, Poule d'Essai des Poulains, Prix de Diane, and Prix Royal Oak.

left: *The celebrated racehorse Red Rum was victorious over the Grand National course a record three times.*

1925. He held the title a record 26 times, but the Derby eluded him until he won on Pinza during his final attempt in 1953. Two years earlier, Ascot had introduced the King George VI and Queen Elizabeth Stakes, the midseason middle-distance championship of Europe. Notable horses to have completed the double in the Derby and the King George include Nijinsky (1970), Mill Reef (1971), Grundy (1975), Troy (1979), Shergar (1981), Nashwan (1989), and Generous (1991).

Outstanding among the champion jockeys after Gordon Richards was the taciturn and impassive Lester Piggott, who was only 18 when he won his first Derby on Never Say Die in 1954. Peerless on the switchback Epsom course, Piggott won the Derby a record nine times. While Piggott was at the peak of his career, the English parliament established the Horserace Betting Levy Board in 1961. The body was empowered to raise a levy from the betting turnover to provide a vital income for racing.

royal winners

In England, Sandown Park in Surrey opened as the first entirely enclosed course in 1875, the year after Fred Archer, the first jockey to capture the public imagination, became champion at only 17 years of age. He retained the title until committing suicide, heartbroken over the death of his young wife and desperately ill from trying to maintain a racing weight, at the age of 29 in 1886. Late in 1897, Tod Sloan, born in Indiana, arrived in England to revolutionize race riding by introducing the "monkey up the stick" seat with short stirrup leathers. The same year the barrier start was introduced and the public followed the popular colors of the Prince of Wales, who won the Derby with Persimmon (1896) and Diamond Jubilee (1900), then as Edward VII with Minoru in 1909.

the sport in the twentieth century

Among the well-known owners during the early part of the twentieth century were the Seventeenth Earl of Derby, who won 19 classics, the Fifth Earl of Rosebery, a former prime minister, and the Aga Khan; who became involved in racing on a large scale in 1922. The first of his five Derby winners was Blenehim in 1930.

Outstanding among the horses in the United States in that era was Man O'War, winner of 20 of 21 races. In addition to breaking five record times, he won the Preakness Stakes by 20 lengths in 1920.

The Cheltenham Gold Cup (3.5 m/5.6 km), Britain's supreme championship for steeplechasers, was instituted in 1924. The first of the great winners was Dorothy Paget's Golden Miller, successful five times between 1932 and 1936 and also winner of the Grand National in 1934. The greatest winner of the Gold Cup since 1945 was the Irish-trained Arkle, who won in 1963, 1965, and 1966. Indifferent to weight and distance, Arkle carried 175 lbs (79.5 kg) to win both the Hennessy Gold Cup in 1964 and 1965 and the Whitbread Gold Cup in 1965.

Gordon (later Sir Gordon) Richards became champion jockey on the flat in

below: *The Cheltenham Festival includes the much coveted Gold Cup, the supreme race for steeplechasers.*

Red Rum became the first horse to win the Grand National three times, his third victory coming in 1977. The same year, Hatta became the first winner owned by Sheikh Mohammed of Dubai, who would soon have about 300 horses in training. He or his Godolphin operation was the leading owner 11 times between 1985 and 1998.

The Jockey Club relinquished much of its responsibility in 1994 when the British Horseracing Board became the supreme authority for the sport.

point-to-pointing

Point-to-pointing is an amateur sport that evolved from the hunting field like National Hunt racing. Contests were set up to race to and from certain points in hunt country, and so the sport got its name. Although it is amateur in name, the sport has become highly organized and professional and has a dedicated following of owners, riders, and spectators. It retains its strong links with hunting; about 200 meetings are run by hunts during the season, which runs from January to June. There are more than 120 point-to-point courses in England and Wales.

Before being eligible to enter a point-to-point competition, a horse must qualify by going out hunting. A horse can then enter any relevant race at any point-to-point, and is entitled to enter its qualifying hunt's members' race. Many successful National Hunt horses, as well as jockeys, have gained valuable experience on the point-to-point circuit.

The sport is popular in Ireland but less so elsewhere. In the United States, amateurs compete in what are known as timber races—over fixed timber obstacles—the most well known of which is the 4-mile (6.4-km) Maryland Hunt Cup. Timber racing has recently become a fixture in Britain, with the Marlborough Cup final being held annually at Barbary Castle in Wiltshire.

below: *While remaining an amateur sport, point-to-pointing is highly competitive, with some races being run annually in England and Wales.*

hunting

Although hunting has been documented and illustrated for many centuries, fox hunting is a comparatively modern sport. It dates from the mid-eighteenth century, when influential breeders started to develop hounds to catch foxes in the open. Until then, the principal quarries for hounds had been deer and hare, and fox hunting was just a form of vermin control.

The old style of fox hunting was to follow a fox's scent, or "drag," to its den and dig it out. Men like Hugo Meynell, master of the Quorn Hunt in 1753, introduced speed, stamina, and drive to the foxhound to augment its existing talents—a good cry and excellent scenting ability.

Today there are about 185 foxhound packs registered in Britain. The sport's governing body is the Master of Foxhounds Association. The packs use different types of hounds, depending on the country that is to be hunted.

While hunting originated in Britain, the sport is also practiced in Australia, New Zealand, the United States, and in parts of Europe, where drag hunting—hounds following a scent laid by a runner—is popular. In France, for example, wild boar, hare, and deer hunting are still enjoyed. A blood horse (i.e., one that is almost clean-bred) is the most popular mount because it can endure the strenuous chase associated with this type of sport.

In Australia and New Zealand the Thoroughbred is the most popular mount because it is best suited to the quarry and terrain the sportsman will encounter.

In the United States, fox hunting follows a pattern similar to Britain's, and the Thoroughbred is again the most popular mount.

A hunt is run by a master, or by a joint-mastership, who provides the money for the hunt and liaises with farmers and landowners over whose land the hunt will pass. The master may be the huntsman, too, responsible for the breeding and hunting of hounds. If this is the case, the hunt employs a kennel-huntsman to take care of the hounds in the kennels and act as whipper-in, or assistant, to the huntsman during a meet. If the master does not hunt hounds, the hunt appoints a huntsman to be responsible for the care and management of the pack.

matching animals to the game

Hounds are usually divided into dog or bitch packs and are hunted on separate days. The ideal hound should be close-coupled with a fairly straight underline and stand about 23 inches (58.4 cm) at the shoulder. Breeders cross different types of dog to get the right hound for a particular type of country.

on foot using beagles, which are smaller than foxhounds.

A suitable mount for hunting must carry its rider safely across country, so it needs stamina, speed, and a natural jumping ability. Half-bred (Thoroughbred cross) horses, often with native pony or Irish blood, are now the most common type of mount in the hunting field. The country to be hunted also dictates the type of horse required. A horse with speed and courage is favored where the country is fast with plenty of jumps, whereas a surefooted, sensible mount is preferred on rougher terrain.

A good day's hunt inevitably provides challenges. However, with a sensible approach, courage, and a fit horse, any rider can compete in this sport.

Hunting in Britain is not confined to foxes. Stag hunting is still popular, although it has been affected by a loss of land in the West country, because of a ban on the sport by the National Trust. A specially bred hound, called a staghound, is used for hunting this quarry. Hares are hunted

harness racing

The sport of harness racing enjoys huge support around the world, especially in the United States, Australia, New Zealand, and Europe, where it often enjoys greater prominence than traditional ridden racing. In England the sport has yet to attain this level of popularity but it is becoming more widely appreciated.

In harness racing the horse races at either a pace or a trot and is controlled by a rider who sits in a lightweight, two-wheeled cart, known as a sulky, which is usually built of aluminum. Pacers and trotters are also raced under saddle, with the jockey adopting a much more upright stance than in traditional racing. France, where the first trotting race was ridden rather than driven, holds the most valuable contest for ridden trotters, the Prix de Cornulier.

pacing and trotting

The two permitted gaits in harness racing are pacing and trotting. The former is a lateral gait where the near and fore legs on both sides move simultaneously. Pacers wear light straps, known as hobbles, that connect the legs on the same side and encourage the horse to maintain this lateral gait. Pacing is marginally faster than trotting and the horse is less likely to break out of the gait. Pacing races are more popular in the United States, Australia, New Zealand, and Great Britain.

below: *In many countries the sport of harness racing has more prominence than traditional ridden racing.*

Trotting is a diagonal gait with the horse's near foreleg and off hind leg moving together, followed by the off fore and near hind. It is the preferred gait in harness racing in mainland Europe.

international competitions

While in England the prize money for harness racers remains minimal compared to that available to flat or jump horses, valuable prizes are offered in other parts of the world. Among the most elite races for pacers are the Cane Futurity, Messenger Stakes, and Little Brown Jug, all held in the United States and the equivalent of flat racing's Triple Crown, while the best trotters vie for honors in the famous French Prix d'Amerique and the American trio of the Hambletonian, Yonkers Trot, and Kentucky Futurity.

racing tracks

Racing circuits usually have a grass or all-weather surface, although in England hard tracks are often made of limestone, and the distances vary from country to country. In England tracks are generally about half a mile (800 m) in circumference, but in Europe they tend to be longer—between 0.6 and 1.2 miles (1–2,000 m), the latter being the distance of the famed circuit at the Hippodrome de Vincennes in Paris.

the influence of the American Standardbred

Two of the most enthusiastic exponents of the sport, the United States and France, also produce the two breeds generally used in the sport.

The American Standardbred is the fastest harness-racing horse in the world. It is the breed most widely favored—either purebred or as a cross—and has also been used to increase the speed of other harness-racing breeds. The Standardbred traces back to an English Thoroughbred sire, Messenger, who was exported to the United States in 1788 and remained there for 20 years. Although he only raced at the gallop, Messenger was able to produce good trotting stock and it was his great grandson, Hambletonian, who is credited with having the greatest impact on the breed.

The name Standardbred derives from the set of standards drawn up for inclusion in the register. The original

standards included the requirement that a horse be able to pace or trot one mile (1.6 km) in 2 minutes 30 seconds or less. This time has been reduced as the speed of the breed has increased.

France's contribution to the sport is the French Trotter, which is seen more widely in Europe and especially in its homeland. Before the Trotteur Française Stud Book was largely closed to non-French breeds in the mid-1930s, some Standardbred blood was introduced in an attempt to increase its speed.

Another prominent breed, now mainly confined to its own country, is the Orlov Trotter of Moscow. It enjoyed great fame before the development of the American super-horse. Crossings with the Standardbred have produced the swifter Russian Trotter.

showing

Showing is not a sport in the truest sense, but a discipline that has gained a huge following in Britain and other countries, such as the United States and Australia. While critics argue that there is no skill involved, it is generally agreed that a high level of horsemanship is required to produce and exhibit horses and ponies in top-class showing. Because it is a subjective art, judging has attracted criticism over the years; judges need to be skilled in order to spot the winning qualities of movement, proportions, and beauty of outline in a show horse or pony.

Shows are run throughout the year by organizations such as the British Show Hack, Cob, and Riding Horse Association, the Sport Horse Breeding Society of Great Britain (formerly the National Light Horse Breeding Society), the National Pony Society, Ponies (UK), and the British Show Pony Society, all of which hold their own championships. Competitors around the world enter their Arabs—whether purebred, crossed with Thoroughbred, or at least a quarter Arab part-bred—into Arab Horse Society classes.

horse classes

Traditionally the most prestigious of all showing categories is those for hunters, both in-hand and ridden. In-hand includes sections for yearlings, two- and three-year-olds, and broodmares, while ridden hunters are divided into eight classes with three weight divisions: light, middle, and heavy. The weight divisions refer to the weight that the horse is able to carry, which is linked to the amount of bone it possesses (measured around the cannon bone).

Other classes include small hunters—15.2 hands high (62.2 ins; 158 cm) or less—; ladies' hunters (ridden sidesaddle); novices; four-year-olds; and working hunters. In the United States all classes jump; in Britain only working hunters must complete a course of natural fences. Ridden hunters are shown at all paces, including the gallop; they are also shown stripped of their tack, are run up in-hand, and in Britain are ridden by a judge.

Hacks are probably one of the most elegant of all show-ring exhibits. They are shown in two height classes, small (14.2–15.2 h.h./58.25–62.2 ins; 148–158 cm) and large (15–15.3 h.h/60.2–63.4 ins; 153–161 cm).

above: *Showing may look relatively easy, but a high level of horsemanship is required to succeed in top level competition.*

left: *Classes for hunters—both ridden and in-hand—remain the most prestigious of all showing categories.*

Riding horses, by definition all-around horses that anyone can ride, are also divided by height: small (14.2–15.2h.h./58.25–62.2 ins; 148–158 cm) and large (over 15.2 h.h./62.2 ins; 158 cm). Cobs must not exceed 15.1 hands high (61.4 ins; 156 cm) and are divided into lightweight and heavyweight classes.

showing ponies

Showing categories for ponies are numerous, but are usually divided between show ponies, working hunters, show hunters, and mountain and moorland (native) breeds. Show ponies are a type, rather than breed, and often look like miniature Thoroughbreds.

Pony classes include lead-rein and first-ridden and are divided into three height categories: 12.2 h.h. (50.4 ins; 128 cm), 13.2 h.h. (54.3 ins; 138 cm), and 14.2 h.h. (58.25 ins; 148 cm). There are nine native pony breeds. These are either shown in individual breed sections or general mountain and moorland classes.

turnout

There are general guidelines for turnout of horse and rider, though it varies depending on the class. Hunters should be shown in a double bridle with a plain noseband and browband, while hacks wear a double bridle but may have a colored browband. A straight-cut showing saddle is ideal because it shows off the horse's

shoulder; more important, the size of the saddle should match the size of the horse. Hunters, hacks, and riding horses are shown with plaited manes and pulled or plaited tails. Cobs are shown with hogged manes, and native breeds are shown in their natural state.

Riders wear tweed jackets (women may wear black or blue); fawn or buff breeches (not white); long boots; a collar and tie; and string or leather gloves. Children wear navy jackets in show pony classes but follow adult dress in other classes. A riding hat and a safety harness is compulsory for all children's and some adult classes.

below: *Working hunters are required to tackle a course of natural-looking fences.*

carriage driving

Carriage driving is a relatively recent arrival on the competitive sports circuit. Although the first international driving championships took place in 1971, the tradition of horse driving has a long history. Chariot races preceeded ridden races by several centuries, and the adaptation and development of harnesses and carriages began as long ago as 250 B.C.

Driving as a pastime came to the fore in Europe during the seventeenth and eighteenth centuries. There are historical records of carriage races with wagers on speed and endurance. The Prince of Wales, the Prince Regent, enjoyed the sport and his enthusiasm made driving fashionable.

At the beginning of the nineteenth century, the arrival of the railroad heralded an end to coach and horse travel, and driving clubs were formed to preserve the skills of four-in-hand coaching. The Coaching Club of Great Britain, formed in 1871, is still in existence today, and coaching classes continue to be a spectacular feature at shows.

below: *Britain's George Bowman and his team of Cumberland cobs competing in the dressage phase of the international driving trials held at Royal Windsor.*

In the twentieth century, the advent of automobiles meant the end of horse-drawn transport on the roads. Nevertheless, pleasure driving has always had supporters, and a small, dedicated band of enthusiasts has ensured that the skills and carriages are preserved. After the Second World War, driving regained some of its popularity, and in 1957, the British Driving Society (BDS) was formed to promote the sport. The society remains strong today and area commissioners organize a range of activities to suit the needs of all levels of driver. In addition to competitive driving trials, there are private classes where the emphasis is on turnout and training. These are held at most horse shows, and an annual summer event is hosted by the BDS.

driving trials

The popularity of horse driving trials is largely attributable to HRH Prince Philip, the Duke of Edinburgh. In 1969, in his capacity as president of the Fédération Equestre Internationale (FEI), the Duke drew up the first rules for horse-driving trials. These were closely based on the format for three-day eventing. The Duke has continued his close association with the sport and currently competes on the national circuit with his team of Fell ponies.

A full horse-driving trials event consists of three separate phases, or competitions. The first phase (A) is a driven dressage test. Phase B is a cross-country marathon, usually 15.5 miles (25 km), in which drivers negotiate eight obstacles against the clock. The final phase is the cone-driving section. The winner is the driver who incurs the fewest penalties in all three sections.

international competition

The first horse driving trials European Championships took place in 1971 in Hungary, and the inaugural World Competition was held in Germany the following year. Although these events were initially restricted to teams of horses, the sport's popularity soon meant that pony teams and pairs, tandems, and singles of both horses and ponies were competing on the international stage.

In 1995 a European Championship for pony teams was held for the first time. In 1998 single horse drivers, who probably make up the largest group of competitors in all driving nations, finally gained their own world event.

The World Four-in-Hand Championships are held bi-annually, as are World Championships for horse pairs and single horses, and the European Championships for pony team driving.

Carriage driving now has an international following. Competitions are held all over the world, and often as many as 18 nations take part. While the sport has, for many years, been dominated by Hungary, other countries—including Switzerland, Germany, the Netherlands, the United States, Great Britain, Belgium, Sweden and Austria—are now forces to be reckoned with.

However, no one country dominates the sport. For example, although the Netherlands, Germany, and Sweden triumphed in the 1998 World Four-in-Hand Championships, only the Netherlands featured at the World Pairs Championships, finishing behind Great Britain and Austria. And at the World Singles Championship, Sweden and the United States took gold and silver, with the Netherlands gaining the bronze.

polo

With its origins in central Asia some 2,000 years ago, polo—a game played on horseback with a stick and a ball—is believed to be the oldest equestrian sport in the world. In the fourteenth century, legend has it that the soldiers of Tamerlane played polo with the heads of their enemies. When heads were in short supply, they played with a ball made of leather.

The game spread across Asia to Mongolia where it was called "pulu," meaning a root, from which the polo ball was made. Muslim invaders from the northwest and the Chinese from the east introduced the game to India. The British discovered the game in India during the nineteenth century. British soldiers played in polo matches and continued to play when they returned home.

the early days

Polo was first played on British soil in 1869 by the 10th Hussars, stationed at Hounslow in Middlesex, England. The earliest matches were played at Hounslow and in Richmond Park, Surrey, and on a small ground near Earl's Court in London. The first country club was the Monmouthshire Polo Club, formed in 1872.

Four years after the first games were played, a match was held at Hurlingham in London. This venue became the headquarters of polo, and in 1875 the Hurlingham Polo Committee (HPC) drew up the first English rules. This committee originally fixed the height of polo ponies at 14 hands. This was later increased to 14.2 hands, and the height ruling was eventually abolished after the First World War. In 1925 the HPC renamed itself the Hurlingham Polo Association (HPA), and this same organization governs the sport in Britain and Ireland today.

the game

A polo team consists of four players. The number four member is often referred to as a back, and is the equivalent of a soccer team's goalkeeper. The best players are usually in positions two and three; these players score most of the goals. In many cases one of the team members is also the patron, the person who finances the team.

at the Guards Polo Club in Windsor Great Park where Britain take on a visiting nation to play for the Coronation Cup. Every four years, Britain and the United States play for an alternative trophy, the Westchester Cup. At another important fixture, the British Open Championships final at Cowdray Park, high-goal teams battle it out in a series of league matches to reach the final.

Although polo is seen as a sport of the rich and privileged, it is increasingly popular at all levels of society. Each year, more clubs request affiliation with the HPA, many universities create their own clubs, and the Pony Club Polo Championships expand. There is an international women's polo organization and there are women's national and international tournaments.

A new version of the game is evolving. Called arena polo, it can be played all year round on an all-weather surface. In arena polo there are often just three players on a team; the ball is larger than a normal polo ball and is of a reflective color.

Polo matches are played in seven-minute chukkas, with four or six chukkas per match. The games are graded into low-, medium-, and high-goal. Each player has an individual handicap, which can range from -2 (the worst) to 10. There are few 10-goal players in the world. Most of them are from the United States, Argentina, and other South American countries. From the late 1870s, when the sport was introduced to the United States, it reigned supreme; but in the 1940s Argentina became the dominant force. Argentina is currently the biggest exporter and breeder of polo ponies in the world.

Today, prestigious polo opens are held in the United States and Argentina. In Britain, one of the highlights of the season is International Day. This is held

left: *In St. Moritz, Switzerland, polo is played in the snow.*

endurance riding

Endurance is the fastest growing equestrian discipline. It was in the spotlight at the end of 1998, when the world championship in Dubai became the Fédération Equestre Internationale's largest-ever championship event, attracting 37 nations.

Although still in its infancy compared to other equestrian sports, endurance riding has acquired a healthy following, especially in the United States, where the sport originated over forty years ago.

In 1955, the first Tevis Cup (named after the president of Wells Fargo) was awarded in honor of the animals and riders of the Pony Express. The race followed the original nineteenth-century route across the Sierra Nevada mountains and had to be completed in a single day. This was so popular that within a decade the sport of endurance riding had been established internationally.

The modern development of Endurance riding began in the 1970s, when several European countries held rides; in 1981 it was recognized as an official sport. By 1979, the need to

below: *ELDRIC was formed in 1979 to bring uniform conduct to the sport.*

balance the test of stamina with welfare considerations saw the formation by seven countries—Britain, France, Germany, Italy, Portugal, Spain, and Switzerland—of ELDRIC, the European Long Distance Rides Conference. ELDRIC formulated rules and gradually brought uniform conduct to the sport. By the 1990s, ELDRIC had expanded to include Argentina, Canada, New Zealand, South Africa, and the United States.

The first European Endurance Championship was held in 1984. Two years later the United States held the first North American championship; the same year, the sport's first World Championship was held in Rome. Stockholm was the venue for the first World Equestrian Games endurance contest in 1990, won by Britain. The other significant international competition—the ELDRIC Trophy, instituted in 1980—has been won nine times by riders from Great Britain, with Germany producing three winners and France two.

Three organizations in Britain are responsible for the sport: the British Endurance Riding Association (BERA), Endurance Horse and Pony Society (EHPS), and Scottish Endurance Riding Club (SERC). BERA offers a range of rides, from 15-mile "pleasure rides" to the highly competitive 100-mile race rides.

the leading endurance rides and riders

A highlight of the calendar in the United Kingdom is the Golden Horseshoe Ride, which covers 100 miles across Exmoor and is run as a competition against the course's conditions, rather than as a race between competitors. A gold award is made to the riders whose horses complete the course in the optimum time under the conditions.

Arab horses have dominated the sport since its inception. The breed's natural stamina and conformation make it generally unbeatable. One horse that did was Jackie Taylor's ELDRIC Trophy winner Sally, a home-bred Trakhener.

In the United States, native breeds such as the Appaloosa, Morgan, and Standardbred are popular choices for many riders and trainers.

Endurance horses generally take time to mature—at the higher echelons of the sport, they take an additional three years to reach their peak. As a consequence, the tendency has been for riders to develop a partnership with one horse and for certain horses to dominate the scene for several years, as in the case of Jill Thomas and her purebred Arab Egyptian Khalifa, European Champions in 1993.

While Britain dominated in the early years, the United States caught up quickly, adapting and devising new techniques for training and management of the horse during races to radically improve speeds. Leading riders who have led the way include Becky Hart with R.O. Grand Sultan, and Valerie Kanavy, twice World Champion.

The sport came of age in 1998 and appeared to reach a crossroads, with growing interest in endurance from the Gulf States. Racing aficionado Sheikh Mohammed of Dubai completed a period of massive financial investment through sponsorship of rides and the development of facilities in Dubai, by putting his muscle behind the sport, literally. He led his country's team and competed in the first 100-mile world championship across the desert.

pony club

The British Pony Club provides the perfect grounding for a future involvement in equestrian sports; it is also a great way to improve a young person's horsemanship while having fun. The Pony Club was founded in 1929 by the Institute of the Horse with the aim of promoting the sport to young people and providing additional instruction. The idea caught on, and within two years there were 59 branches and about a thousand members. The Pony Club continued to grow in strength and had burgeoned to more than 165 branches with 17,000 members by the end of the Second World War.

The Pony Club is a registered independent charity and today has 364 branches and about 36,000 members.

It also operates outside the UK, with branches in more than 16 countries worldwide. Members pay an annual subscription to the local branch; this entitles the child to membership in the club as a whole.

The Pony Club remains true to its original aims and is open to anyone up to the age of 21 who owns, or has

access to, a pony. Each branch of the Pony Club organizes a full program of rallies, competitions, social events, visits, and an annual camp, most of which are held when school is not in session. Annual camps are held in locations that offer suitable accommodation for both ponies and children, and include a mix of tuition, fun events, and competitions.

Pony Clubs set efficiency tests to encourage general improvement in

right: *An ideal mounted games pony should be fast, intelligent, and agile.*

left: *Pony Clubs from around the world unite at a Eurocamp.*

standards of horsemanship. The tests, beginning at the most basic level, are D, D+, C, C+, B, H, and A. Grade A is a very high standard and is achieved by relatively few members. A road safety exam is taken by members before they attempt test C and above.

the Pony Club's sporting calendar

Each Pony Club branch runs competitive events. Teams are entered into area competitions and the winners, in turn, qualify for the annual Pony Club Championships. The competitions at this level include horse trials, dressage, show jumping, and tetrathlon (which consists of running, riding, shooting, and swimming). The tetrathlon was originally designated as a competition

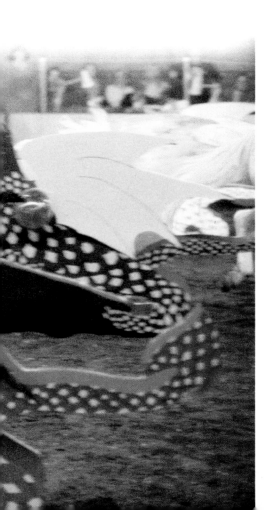

for boys, but was soon opened up to include both sexes.

Depending on the branch's access to a polo ground, Pony Club members may also play polo. There is an annual polo competition divided into age groups. The Pony Club has also taken up the relatively new sport of polocrosse, a combination of polo and lacrosse in which riders use a long stick with a net on the end to pick up and pass the ball.

Probably the best known Pony Club competition is the Prince Philip Mounted Games Championship, instigated by HRH Prince Philip in 1957. This requires teams of riders to compete in a number of gymkhana games. Points are awarded for each

game and accumulated for a final score. Branches compete in area and zone finals, and a grand finale is held annually at the Horse of the Year Show in London. While this sport does not require a pony of great breeding, the animal must be agile, intelligent, obedient, and fast. Increased professionalism within the games means that experienced mounted games ponies can change hands at increasingly exorbitant prices.

Although the Pony Club has had strong links with hunting in the past, it is gradually loosening its ties with this activity. Traditionally the names of the individual branches of the Pony Club were based on hunt counties and hunts still organize Pony Club or children's meets. The Pony Club remains the ideal breeding ground for future equestrian stars and provides an ideal environment for pony and child to learn and grow together.

left: *Pony Club members battle it out in the final of the Prince Philip Mounted Games Championship held at the Horse of the Year Show in London.*

western sports

The rodeo, where the modern-day American cowboy demonstrates his prowess with horse and rope, evolved during the nineteenth century. The name "rodeo" comes from the Spanish, meaning "to round up."

At early rodeos, ranchers gambled on displays of ranching skills. In the beginning, these contests took place at random in the main streets of towns. The first commercial rodeo event took place in Colorado in 1888. Today the rodeo is a thriving business, with big prize money offered to those brave cowboys, and cowgirls, willing to risk life and limb.

classic competitions

There are five classic events included in every rodeo, some of which have their origins in ranch work. Calf roping involves the roping and tying up of a calf. The animal is given several seconds' head start before rider and horse enter the ring to pursue it. The cowboy lassoes his quarry and secures the rope to the horn of his saddle. The horse is specially trained to step backward to keep the rope taut and, in this way, the calf is restrained. The rider flips the calf onto its side and secures three of its legs with a short length of rope. If the calf escapes within five seconds the contestant is disqualified; the competition is based on time.

In the saddle-bronc contest, riders are allocated their horses and the order of competition is set by lottery. The horse wears a modified stock saddle, without the horn. A piece of rope is attached to the horse's halter as reins, and a strap is tightened around its flanks to encourage bucking. The rider wraps the rope around one hand and places his spurs on the horse's shoulders. He uses the spurs as he is released from the gates and into the arena. The ride must last 10 seconds and marks are awarded for the performance of both rider and horse.

In the bareback bronc competition the rider must remain astride his mount, using just one hand to hold onto the grip, which is attached to a strap around the horse's girth. In this event, as in bullriding, the contest must

left: *In the bareback bronc contest, the rider must remain astride his mount for eight seconds.*

right: *The rodeo contest originated in the nineteenth century and has become a thriving business across America.*

last for eight seconds. In bull riding the cowboy is allowed to use two hands on the girth grip, but it is even more important that he remain onboard because a bull, given the opportunity, will gore an unseated rider.

In steer wrestling, the cowboy gallops after a steer, with another cowboy riding alongside to ensure that the animal keeps a straight course. When the first rider draws even with the steer he jumps off his horse, grabs the steer by the horns, and wrestles it to the ground. Time is the deciding factor in this contest. Other rodeo contests include barrel racing for cowgirls, team roping, and chuck-wagon racing.

Western riding classes

An equally popular but considerably less dangerous pastime is Western-style riding. Classes in Western-style riding are held at horse shows across the United States. This area of showing, where competitors adopt the stock-seat style, is divided into four categories. Most horse breeds may compete in all four, although the most popular choices of mount include American Saddlebreds, Arabs, and Morgans.

In the Western pleasure section, a horse is shown at walk, jog (slow trot), lope (slow canter), and hand gallop. A horse competing in a reining (or stock) class must perform a series of patterns, including spins, sliding stops, and circles, to demonstrate obedience and rapport with its rider.

The working-cow class involves, as the title suggests, working a cow to specific criteria, and the horse undertakes a series of tasks to achieve this. The aim of the trail-horse class is to negotiate a series of natural obstacles, including water, logs, and gates.

turnout

Correct turnout for Western-style classes includes a stock saddle and bridle with a curb bit or hackamore. Horses are shown with long or shortened manes and full tails. Riders wear traditional Western riding gear, comprising a broad-brimmed hat, shirt, pants, chaps, and cowboy boots.

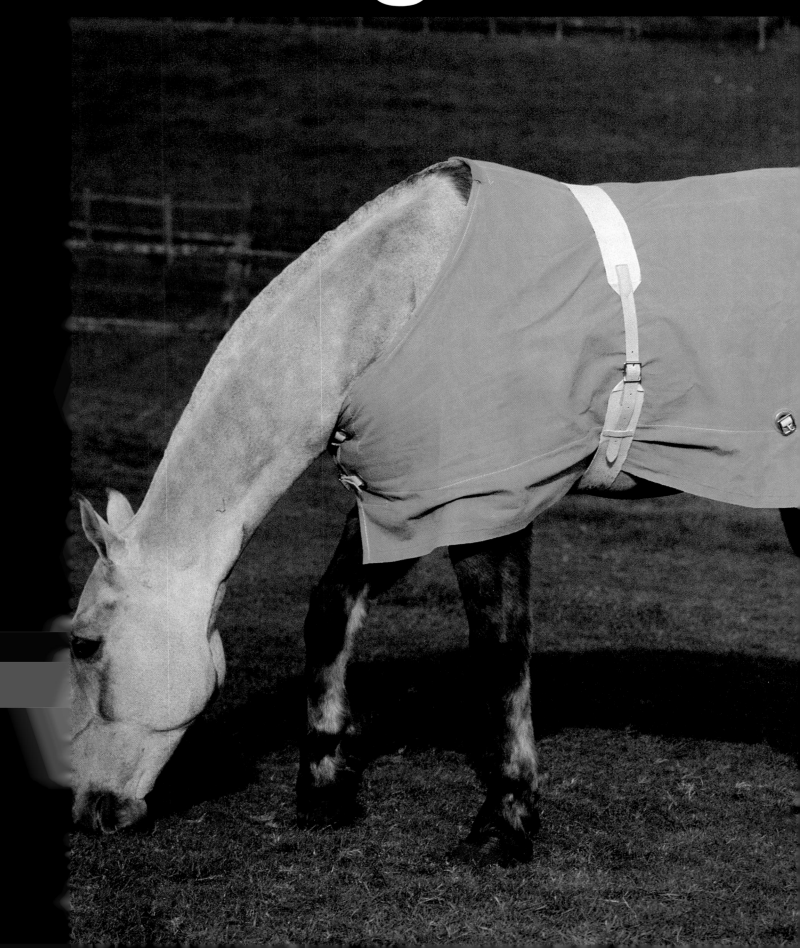

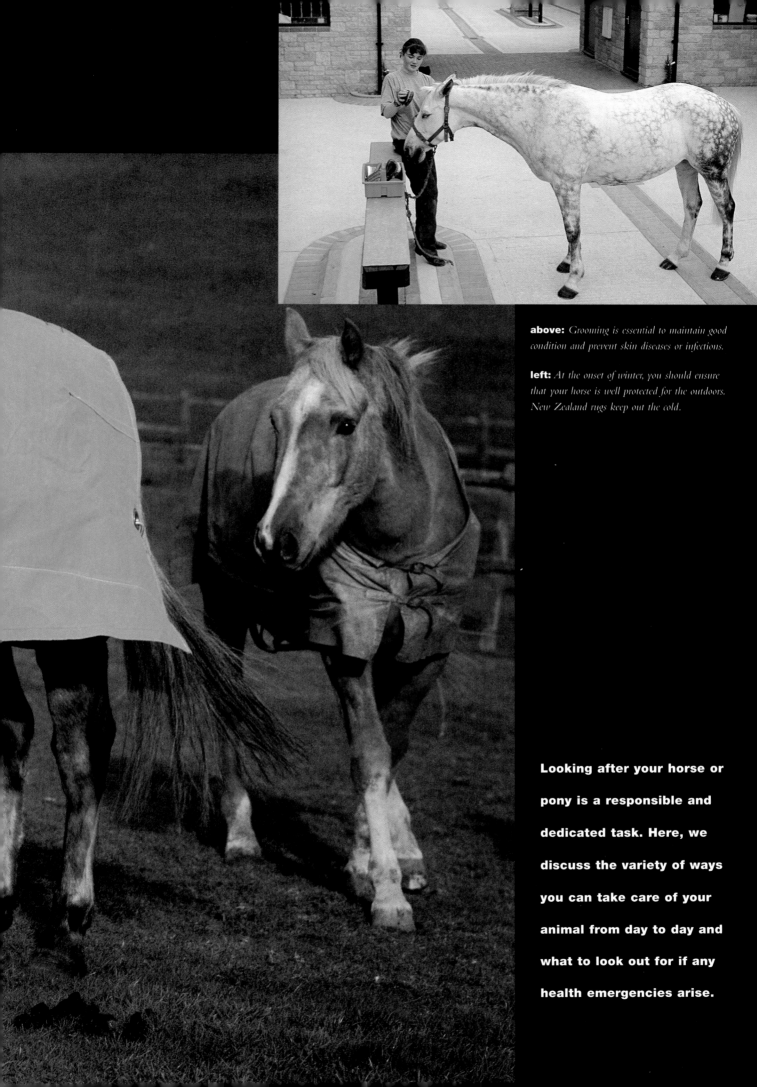

above: *Grooming is essential to maintain good condition and prevent skin diseases or infections.*

left: *At the onset of winter, you should ensure that your horse is well protected for the outdoors. New Zealand rugs keep out the cold.*

Looking after your horse or pony is a responsible and dedicated task. Here, we discuss the variety of ways you can take care of your animal from day to day and what to look out for if any health emergencies arise.

feeding

In its natural, undomesticated state a horse would spend a large proportion of its day feeding, moving from place to place to find new grass and plants. If food was not plentiful the horse would lose condition and regain it when more food became available.

The horse's digestive system evolved to fit this pattern of grazing little and often. It has a relatively small stomach (with a capacity of 17–30 pints/8–14 liters, depending on the size of the horse) in comparison to the size of its large intestine. A horse's stomach works best when it is only three-quarters full. Any feeding regime should imitate the natural pattern as closely as possible to allow the horse to gain maximum benefit from the food it consumes.

A horse required to work cannot consume sufficient bulk food at one time to replace the energy it has used. Therefore small amounts of energy-giving foods, known as concentrates, are required in addition. The precise ratio of bulk to concentrates depends on the amount and type of work the horse is required to do and on the animal's individual needs.

Feeding a horse successfully requires knowledge of its digestive system and the nutritional value of different foods.

left: *A horse should have access to fresh water at all times.*

It is also necessary to judge the correct diet for a horse of a particular size, age, and build, and doing a particular job. Every horse is different and its feeding regime should be tailored to meet its specific needs.

what to feed

Basically a horse's diet should consist of water, bulk food (roughage), and concentrates. Fresh water should be available at all times. The percentage of water in a horse's body is high—as much as 80 percent in a young horse and around 60 percent in an adult horse. The amount of water needed by a horse will depend on several factors, including its age, the sort of work it is doing, the type of food it is eating, and the external temperature.

bulk food

Bulk food, also known as roughage or forage, is fed as grass, hay, or hay replacers. Hay falls into two categories: seed hay, made from grasses specifically sown as an annual crop, or meadow hay, cut from permanent pasture. Other forms of bulk food include haylage, which is preserved forage sold in sealed plastic bags, and chaff or chop, which is hay that has been chopped into small pieces, either on its own or mixed with a small proportion of oat straw. This is often added to concentrates to aid digestion.

concentrates

Concentrates give energy and are fed in small amounts. There are a great variety of these energy-giving foods available, including cereals and compound feeds. The latter contain a number of ingredients and are specially formulated to provide a balanced diet.

Oats: Oats are considered to be a good all-around feed, although they can cause some horses to "hot up"—become overexcitable. Oats are fed bruised, rolled, or crushed to make the grains more easily digested. Once this process has taken place they must be used within two to three weeks.

below: *The main part of a horse's diet should consist of bulk food, in the form of hay, hay replacers, or grass.*

Barley: Barley has a high energy value and is fed cracked, rolled, flaked, or micronized (cooked). It can also be fed as a mash; this is prepared by adding boiling water to flaked barley and leaving it to cool. Whole barley can only be fed if it is boiled first.

Maize: Maize has a high carbohydrate content, but is low in protein and fiber. It is fed flaked or micronized. It can cause horses to "hot up" and is therefore used sparingly.

Bran: Bran has a high fiber content and can be fed dry in small quantities, mixed with other feed or as a mash. Bran adds bulk to the diet and aids digestion.

Linseed: Linseed is the seed of the flax plant and is poisonous if not boiled first. It is rich in oil and helps promote a shiny coat. Linseed is added to the diet either as a jelly or a gruel (tea).

Sugar beet: Sugar beet has a high fiber and sugar content and is an energy-producing feed that is very palatable. Sugar beet comes in either pulp or cube form and must be soaked for at least 12 hours (longer for cubes) before feeding.

compounds

A compound feed is a scientifically formulated mixture of ingredients, including added vitamins and minerals, that provides a balanced diet to complement forage. Compounds come in either cube (or nut) form, or as a coarse mix. They are available in a variety of grades to suit all types of horses and ponies.

Salt: Salt is an essential part of the horse's diet and is best provided as a salt lick. This is placed in a specially designed container on the stable wall so that the horse has easy access to it.

Succulents: Roots and fruits, such as carrots and apples, added to the diet make the feed more appetizing.

Supplements: A wide range of supplements are available to provide the horse with vitamins and minerals. It is best to get expert advice before making a choice.

Ways to feed: Concentrates should be given to a horse in a feed manger or a plastic or rubber feed bowl. The latter method can be wasteful, since the horse may tip it over. Mangers or bowls should be cleaned thoroughly every day. Hay is best fed from a hay net or a hay rack (the former is more practical, as the height can be adjusted to suit different horses).

Storage: Ideally, feed should be stored in a clean feed room in dry, rodent-proof containers. Buy only enough for a two- or three-week supply, since feed deteriorates if kept for long periods.

left: Salt is an essential part of a horse's diet and is best provided as a salt lick.

opposite (left to right): The variety of horse feeds available today is enormous. These are the staple types that can vary a horse's diet. **1** *bran;* **2** *course mix;* **3** *meadow and seed hay;* **4** *crushed oats;* **5** *sugar beet (shreds/nuts/soaked);* **6** *whole barley;* **7** *flaked maize;* **8** *horse and pony nuts.*

general management of the horse

Horses are grazing animals used to large, open spaces and companionship of other horses. Keeping them in stables, or even at grass where the space they live in will obviously be confined, and on their own, is not natural and therefore whatever system you use to keep your horse you should provide the best and most natural environment possible.

Keeping and owning a horse is a full-time responsibility and it is up to you to ensure that your horse has both its physical and pyschological needs met. A horse must be provided with companionship, both human and equine, and sufficient exercise, whether it be riding or grazing, to keep it from becoming bored and listless.

There are two main management systems for keeping a horse, either grass- or stable-kept, or a combination of the two, the latter of which offers the horse a comparatively natural existence without the need of constant exercise.

livery (boarding stables)

Those who have neither the facilities nor the time to keep their horses at home can use the services of a boarding stable. There are different forms of livery available depending on your budget and how much of the work you are prepared to do. The most common types are full, grass, part, working, and DIY. At one end of the scale there is full livery where the stable does everything including, if necessary, exercising, while at the other end there is the DIY option where you rent a stable and do all the work yourself.

grass-kept horses

pasture

The exact acreage required for a horse at grass depends on the quality of pasture available but as a general rule, if more than one horse is grazed, then one acre per horse is sufficient since this will allow space for grass management. A single horse will require more and, if it is in use year-round, alternative pasture must be found at least for a couple of weeks a year in order for the ground to be rested and for it to remain in good condition. Ideally a suitable field for your horse should be divided into several paddocks so that these can be used in rotation, which will help to maintain the grazing. The field must be checked daily for rubbish, holes in the fencing, and anything else that could cause harm to your horse.

poisonous plants

The field should be checked weekly for poisonous plants, shrubs, or trees. Some

Ragwort

Privet

Laurel

Yew

above: *The field should be securely and safely fenced to prevent the horse from either injuring itself or escaping.*

of these are not palatable but others are and, once tasted, a horse may seek them out. Those that cause the most serious harm to horses include yew, ragwort, deadly nightshade, foxglove, laburnum, oak leaves and acorns, buttercups, bracken, rhododendron, box, privet and laurel, meadow saffron, locoweed, red maple, castor bean, star thistle, horsetail, and sorghum. Plants and shrubs should be dug up and disposed of safely. Trees that cannot be removed should be securely fenced off.

fencing and gates
The field should be safely and adequately fenced so that the horse cannot injure itself or escape. There are several fencing options available and the type of horse you have should be taken into consideration when putting up a fence. A thick hedge is suitable, and will also provide additional shelter, but must not contain any posionous plants. Post-and-rail fencing is secure but expensive, while flexi fencing, using posts and strong, plastic tape, is clearly visible to the horse. Electric fencing or plain wire fencing are also suitable as

long as they are tightly secured to wooden posts, and visible. Barbed wire and mesh fencing, which horses can get their feet caught in, should not be used. Gates should open into the field and should be securely fastened.

shelter
Adequate shelter is required to protect the horse from wind and rain and sun. Shelter can either take the form of a grove of trees or high hedge, providing it offers protection from the wind, or a specially-built shelter shed. The latter is open at the front and positioned so that a horse cannot get trapped

between it and the fence. If there are several horses using the field then the shelter should be of a sufficient size and wide enough to allow access for several horses at once. The back of the shelter should face the prevailing wind.

water
A horse needs access to a constant supply of fresh water. The most effective way of supplying this is by a trough filled from a supply of piped water, although it will require checking at least twice a day in winter to ensure that neither the water nor the supply valve has frozen. A stream is suitable so long as the approach to it is easily accessed and the bottom is gravel and not sand. A bucket, without a handle, and placed inside a tire to keep it from being easily knocked over, can be used but must be checked and refilled at least twice a day.

stabled horses
The type of stable you use for your horse should be both suitable and safe. Stables are normally constructed of wood, concrete blocks, or bricks

below: *The stable should ideally give a view of the other horses, which will provide added stimulation.*

above: *Internal stalls are used in many countries but the buildings must be well-ventilated to limit the spread of contagious diseases.*

top and above: *Good choices of bedding are essential to keep the horse comfortable and injury-free. Shavings make an excellent bedding, while rubber matting is best used in conjunction with another type of bedding on top.*

and must have adequate ventilation. The minimum size for a horse's stable is about 12 feet (3.6 m) square with the opening of the doorway being at least 3.5 feet (1 m) wide and 7 feet (2 m) high. The top part of the door should be hooked back securely while the lower part of the door is secured with bolts top and bottom. The floor of the stable should be hard-wearing and non-slippery with a slight slope for drainage purposes. The roof must be sloped with adequate guttering and downpipes and an overhang to protect the horse, and the inside of the stable, from wind and rain.

The American barn, which holds a number of stables inside a large covered building, is popular in many countries since it provides the horse with company and is particularly useful if extremes of temperature are the norm. However, the building must be adequately ventilated to limit the spread of contagious diseases.

Like the grass-kept horse, the stabled horse requires access to a constant supply of fresh water from a water bucket either on the floor or suspended from the wall. Both will need checking and refilling regularly. A feeding manger should be fitted at the horse's nose level for easy access.

bedding

Bedding provides comfort when the horse is standing all day on a hard floor and acts as a soft bed for it to lie down on. There are several types of bedding available commercially but the comfort of your horse, and any health problems it may have, must be your prime considerations when making your choice.

Straw is traditionally used because it makes the warmest and most comfortable bed and is cheap and easily disposable. However, it may be dusty or contain fungal spores that can lead to respiratory problems. Wheat straw is harder than either barley or oat, which horses may be inclined to eat.

Wood shavings are clean, hygienic, and cannot be eaten. They provide a good alternative for horses with respiratory problems, as long as the

left: *Banking up the bedding around the sides of the stable helps to prevent the horse from getting trapped on its side against the wall.*

shavings are dust free. However, disposal is more difficult since shavings take longer to rot down.

Shredded paper is dust-free and provides a warm bed, but paper disintegrates rapidly once wet.

Hemp is a relatively new form of bedding made from the hemp plant. Initially it is expensive because a lot is required, but once down it is easily managed and is very absorbent.

Rubber matting is best used with a small amount of bedding on top. On its own it affords little comfort, warmth, or protection against a horse becoming cast (trapped on its side against the wall).

mucking out (stable cleaning)

A stable must be mucked out every day and if the horse is stabled all the time, droppings should be removed and the bedding leveled at least three times a day.

To clean a stable out you need a wheelbarrow, a straw or shavings fork, a shovel, and a broom. With a straw bed, a full cleaning should be done once a day. Remove droppings and separate the wet, dirty straw from the clean. Pile the latter up against one wall, tossing it to reveal any hidden droppings, and remove the rest. Sweep the floor and wash it using stable disinfectant. Once the floor is dry, new straw should be added to the clean, but used, material, to make a deep bed. By banking up the bedding around the sides of the stable you will reduce drafts and help to prevent the horse from becoming cast if it lies down or rolls.

If shavings, hemp, or paper bedding is used, droppings and wet parts of the bed must be removed regularly but a full cleaning may be necessary only once or twice a week.

grooming

Each horse should have its own grooming kit to prevent the spread of infections.

A basic grooming kit should comprise the following items: body brush, for removing dust and scurf from coat, mane, and tail; metal curry comb, for cleaning out the body brush; rubber or plastic curry comb, for removing dried-on mud (care should be taken when using these on either particularly thin- or sensitive-skinned horses); a dandy brush for removing heavy dirt and dust, (not to be used on clipped or sensitive horses); a hoof pick for cleaning out the feet; hoof oil for oiling the hooves; plastic mane comb; cotton wool pads or sponges for cleaning the eyes, nose and dock (a separate one is required for each area).

Additional equipment includes a crocus cloth for removing stains, a wisp or massage pad to promote circulation, and stable rubber for the final polish.

Grooming fulfills different purposes depending on whether the horse is stabled or kept at grass. A stabled horse requires daily grooming to

below: *The stable must be mucked out daily and droppings removed regularly throughout the day.*

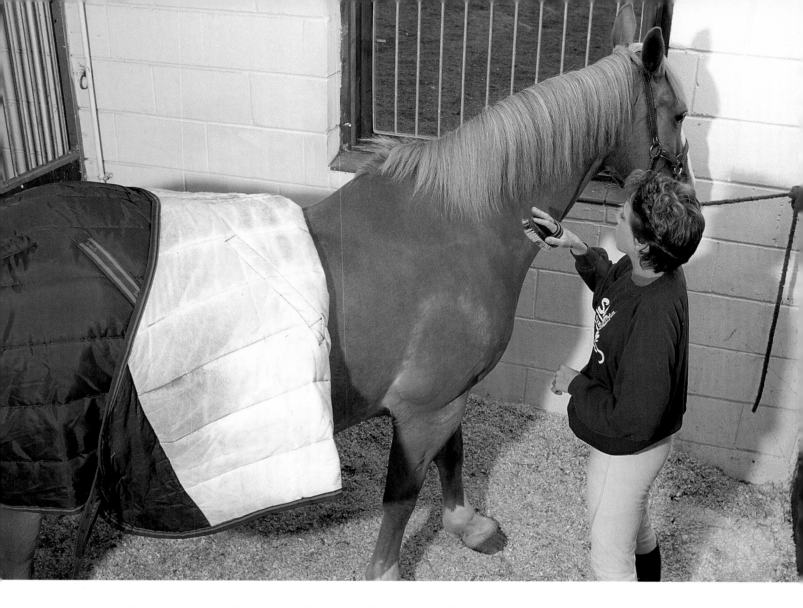

maintain a healthy coat and skin, while a grass-kept horse should have the worst of the mud removed but should not be groomed excessively since this removes essential grease from the coat that keeps the horse warm and dry. However a grass-kept horse should be checked daily, have its feet picked out and its shoes checked, and any mud and sweat marks removed with a dandy brush or rubber curry comb. Its eyes, nose, muzzle, and dock should be sponged out.

above: *A stabled horse requires daily grooming to maintain a healthy coat and skin.*

Quartering is essentially a quick groom to remove stable stains and tidy up the horse before exercise.

Full grooming is generally more effective after exercise when the horse is warm. While everyone has their own methods there are some general guidelines.

Once the horse is tied up, begin by picking out each hoof. Pull the hoof pick down each side of the frog from heel to toe to remove mud and manure. Dried mud can be removed with a dandy brush or rubber curry comb. Holding the body brush in the

left: *A basic grooming kit includes body brushes, sponges, hoof pick and oil, mane comb, rubber curry comb, metal curry comb, sweat scarpu, and stable rubbers.*

hand nearest the horse (with the metal curry comb in the other hand to clean the brush every three to four strokes and by tapping it on a hard surface every so often to dislodge the dirt), begin at the top of the neck using short, strong strokes in the direction of the lay of the coat and work down toward the tail, brushing all parts of the body. Untie the horse before brushing its face, fastening the headstrap around its neck to allow you to clean underneath the straps, and hold onto the rope.

Use the body brush on the mane and tail, being careful not to break the hairs. Hold the tail away from the body and brush out in small sections.

Clean the eyes, muzzle, and dock using individual sponges for each part.

A wisp or massage pad can be used on the neck, shoulders, quarters, thighs, which will help to tone the muscles and improve circulation.

A slightly damp stable rubber wiped over the body will remove any remaining dust. Before applying hoof oil, brush off any mud first. Cover the hoof, from the bulbs of the heel up to the coronet, with a thin layer of oil.

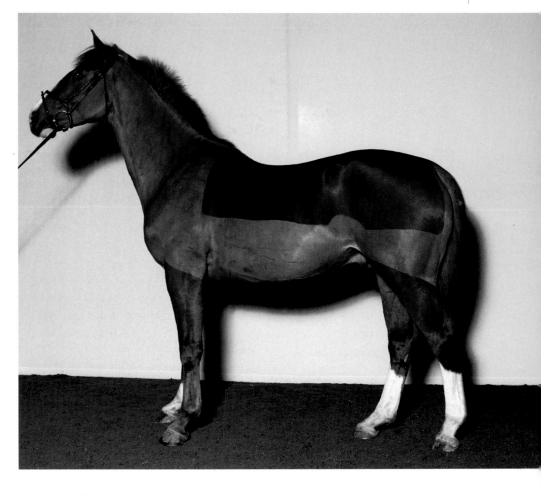

types of clips

Horses grow thicker coats in the winter and may need to be clipped if required to do anything more than

above and below left: *Stabled horses that work are clipped during the winter months to prevent excessive sweating from a heavier coat, which would ultimately lead to loss of condition. Two types of clips often used are the blanket (above) and the hunter (below).*

light work. A horse that sweats excessively will lose condition and runs the risk of catching a chill if not dried properly. Once clipped, a horse will require rugs for extra warmth (see equipment page 155).

The type of clip used will depend on the individual and the work it is expected to do, but the most popular clips are the hunter, where the hair is left on the legs and saddle patch; the blanket, which leaves an area of the horse's back, loins, and quarters unclipped, and also the legs; and the trace, which removes hair from the underside of the neck, between the forelegs, the belly, and upper part of the hind legs.

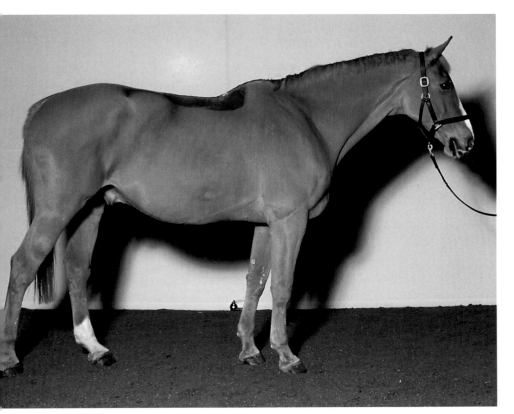

tack and equipment

Saddlery must be correctly fitted so it causes no damage or discomfort to the horse, and must be suitable for the required purpose. A trip to any saddler shows the huge range available, but at the outset the most basic equipment your horse requires is a saddle, bridle, bit, headcollar, and lead rope. Expert advice should be sought to ensure that the tack is the correct fit and safe to use. Saddlery is expensive, but good quality leather tack, if maintained, is a lasting investment. Tack can be bought secondhand or may be sold with the horse, but it must be the correct size and in good condition.

saddles

Saddles are generally constructed from good quality leather—one reason why they are so expensive—although there are some synthetic ones available. The tree—the foundation part of the saddle, made from laminated wood, plastic, or fiberglass—must be the correct width for your horse. When the saddle is on, check that it does not pinch or rub the back and that there is a clear channel so it does not press on the withers or the spine.

The correct way to put on a saddle is to place it forward on the horse before gently sliding it back, to ensure that the

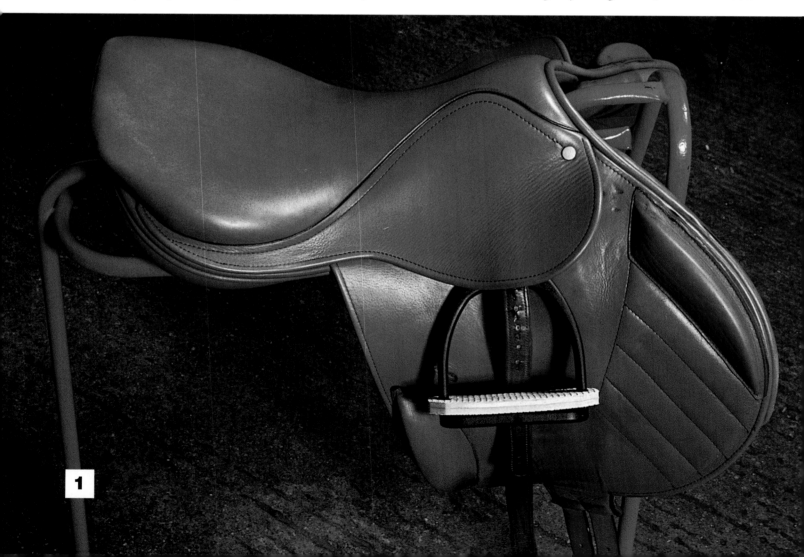

hairs on its back lie flat. The saddle should be placed centrally and in such a position that it does not interfere with the shoulders or put pressure on the loins.

types of saddles

A general-purpose saddle is suitable for all types of riding but there are saddles designed for specific disciplines. A show-jumping saddle has forward-cut flaps and a longer tree, while a dressage saddle has a deeper seat and straighter flaps, and a showing saddle is cut to show off the horse to its best advantage. Racing saddles are lightweight and allow the jockey to ride with short stirrups. A Western saddle, with its distinctive high pommel and cantle, is designed to provide maximum rider comfort.

A numnah or saddle cloth can be used underneath the saddle to give added protection and absorb sweat, but it should never be used to compensate for an ill-fitting or badly stuffed saddle.

1 *Jumping saddle*
2 *Child's saddle*
3 *Dressage saddle*
4 *Flat racing saddle*
5 *General-purpose saddle*
6 *Western Pleasure Show saddle*
7 *Sidesaddle*

girths

The girth keeps the saddle in place. It is therefore essential that it is in good repair and that the stitching is regularly checked. Girths come in a variety of designs and materials, including leather, cotton, wool, web, and nylon.

stirrup irons and leathers

Stirrup irons must be made of stainless steel and should be large enough for the rider's boot, but not so large that the foot can slip through. Rubber treads on the irons help prevent the foot from slipping, and safety irons, often used by children, prevent the foot from becoming trapped. The irons are attached to stirrup leathers, which are fitted onto the bars of the saddle.

bridle

The bridle is constructed of leather and is made up of a headpiece, cheekpieces—the latter are adjustable and attached to the bit—throatlash, to keep the bridle in place, browband, to stop the head piece slipping back, and, usually, a noseband. Reins are made of leather, leather and rubber, or nylon.

bits

There are several types of bits available and the choice depends on the individual horse. The most widely used is the snaffle, which comes in a number of designs, including the straight-bar or mullen-mouth, and the single- or double-jointed. The straight bar puts pressure on the tongue, while the jointed snaffles work on the corners of the mouth as well. There are different designs of cheekpieces, including the egg-butt and loose-ring, the former preventing the horse's lips from being pinched.

The double bridle comprises two bits, both of which have separate reins. A bridoon is a form of snaffle but lighter and with a thinner mouthpiece,

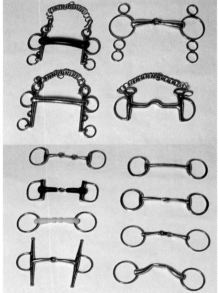

above: *The choice of bits available include the snaffle, the curb bit, and the Kimblewick.*

left: *The double bridle comprises a bridoon and curb bit and chain, and is used with two sets of reins.*

right: *A correctly fitted snaffle bridle with cavesson noseband.*

and a curb bit is used with a curb chain. It should only be used once the horse is going correctly in a snaffle and never by an inexperienced rider.

The Pelham is a combination of the bridoon and curb but on one mouthpiece and is used with two pairs of reins, while the Kimblewick is a single-rein pelham with a straight bar and small tongue groove. A bitless bridle, also known as a hackamore, is designed to work by putting pressure on the horse's nose. It is often used in Western-style riding and requires a special technique.

fitting the bit

Whatever the type of bit, it must be the correct size and at the right height in the horse's mouth. If it is too narrow it pinches the corners of the horse's mouth, while one that is too big causes soreness by unnecessary movement. The tongue should lie comfortably below the bit, which should be of the correct thickness—the thinner the bit, the stronger the pressure. However, if it is too thick, the horse will find it uncomfortable.

left: *A New Zealand rug is an essential piece of equipment for a clipped horse that is kept at grass.*

additional equipment

Leg bandages are used for support, protection against injury, and warmth. Bandages are used with additional padding, such as cotton wool or gamgee, to keep the pressure even and provide additional warmth. They are available with different types of fastening, including tape and Velcro, and must be washed regularly and thoroughly dry before use. Bandages are used to protect the tail when traveling, to keep it clean and encourage hairs to lie flat.

Boots are available in a number of designs to protect the legs from injury and must be fastened securely to prevent chaffing. Brushing boots protect the horse from injuries to the inside of the fetlock from blows from the opposite foot, while tendon boots give protection without restricting movement. Over-reach boots protect the heel and lower part of the pastern from being damaged if struck by the toe of the hind legs. The latter must be correctly fitted so that the horse cannot tread on them. Traveling boots can be used instead of bandages to provide protection when the horse is being transported.

nosebands

There are a number of different types of noseband but the cavesson is probably the most commonly used. It comprises one strip of leather that fits underneath the cheekpieces and can be used with a standing martingale. It is the only type of noseband to use with a double bridle. The dropped noseband sits above the nostrils and fits below the bit, resting on the chin groove. Once fitted, you should be able to fit two fingers beneath it. A flash noseband has two straps, the narrower of which fastens below the bit to prevent a horse from opening its mouth too wide.

martingales

There are two basic types of martingale—the standing and running—both of which are used to provide additional control and prevent the horse from raising its head too high. A standing martingale is fitted to a cavesson noseband and attached to the girth, passing between the forelegs and through a loop on the neck strap, which supports it. The running version is attached to the girth and passes between the forelegs, but then divides in two. Each of the ends are fitted with a ring, through which the reins are passed. It is also supported by a neck strap.

care of tack

Tack needs to be regularly cleaned and checked in order to remain safe to use and comfortable for the horse to wear. After use, the bit should be cleaned and any mud or dirt removed from the saddle and bridle. The girth must be cleaned of sweat and dirt to prevent it from becoming hard and cracked, especially if made of leather. Tack should be taken apart at least once a week and given a thorough cleaning.

rugs

Rugs are essential for clipped horses during the winter months. The type required depends on the individual, the type of clip, and whether the horse is kept inside or out. One that is kept out needs a waterproof canvas New Zealand rug, while a stabled horse requires stable rugs. Rugs are secured by leg straps (in the case of New Zealand rugs), a surcingle, or roller. Other rugs include sweat sheets, to prevent a horse from getting a chill when cooling down, and exercise and summer sheets.

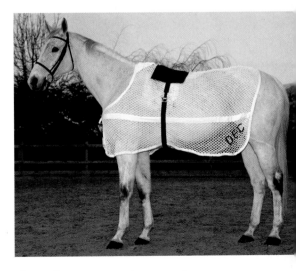

above: *Sweat rugs are used to prevent the horse from getting a chill when cooling down after work.*

shoeing

The need to shoe a horse is a direct result of domestication. In its natural state, the horse has no need for shoes, since its feet wear down at a slower rate than they grow. The level of wear and tear that domestication has placed on a horse's feet means that metal shoes must be fitted to prevent them from wearing down.

Even if a horse is not shod because it is not working or is resting, it still

requires regular visits from the farrier. The horn grows at an average rate of around a tenth to a third of an inch (5–9 mm) per month and most horses need their feet trimmed every four to five weeks, regardless of whether the shoes have worn down, or not. If the shoes are not worn down, they can be refitted. Foals should be seen regularly by the farrier, since many foot problems can be rectified if identified early enough.

shoeing procedures

A farrier will bring a mobile forge with him and employ either the hot- or cold-shoeing method. The hot-shoeing method is considered to be the best since it allows the farrier to

above: *Nails are hammered into the insensitive wall of the foot to keep the shoe in place.*

make minute adjustments and ensures a perfect fit. However, cold-shoeing, where a ready-shaped shoe is nailed to the foot, is acceptable. To shoe a

left: *Shoes are necessary to prevent the horse's hooves from wearing down quicker than they are renewed.*

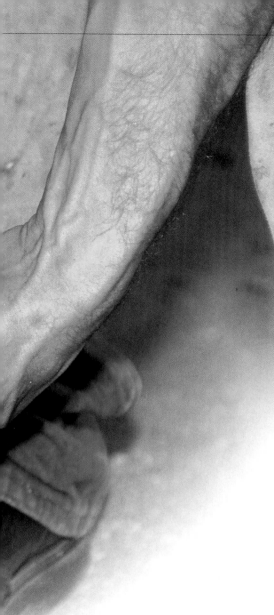

horse, the farrier first removes the old shoes by knocking up the clenches (the turned-over points of the nail) that hold the shoe in place. He then trims excess growth off the hoof wall, cleans it up, and levels it with a rasp.

In the hot-shoe method, the new shoe is heated and placed on the foot for a couple of seconds to ensure that the fitting is correct—this part of the foot has no nerve endings so the horse feels no pain. The shoe is then plunged into cold water before being nailed into place. The ends of the nails, which ideally should exit the hoof about a third of the way up the wall, are bent over to form clenches. The rim of the foot is smoothed with a rasp to eliminate any sharp edges on the clenches.

right: *The farrier uses a rasp to smooth the horn.*

types of shoes

Most horseshoes are made of steel, although race horses are fitted with aluminum shoes called racing plates. Plastic glue-on shoes are used in certain circumstances. Most shoes have a groove, called fullering, on the underside; this makes the shoe lighter and gives it a better grip. There are different types of shoe to suit different activities. For example, a plain, stamped shoe simply fitted with nail holes and a toe clip is only suitable for horses doing slow work.

Shoes on the front feet normally have one toe clip, while shoes on the hind feet have two quarter clips, one on either side of the foot. These clips help to prevent the shoe from moving sideward and allow the farrier to slant the toe slightly. This prevents the horse from over-reaching—striking the heel of the front foot with the toe of the hind shoe.

There is a range of remedial shoes to relieve foot problems caused by malformation, disease (such as laminitis and navicular disease), or injury. One of the most common types is the bar shoe; this has a connecting bar that gives additional support to the back of the foot. There are several variations of this shoe, including the egg-bar and the heart-bar. With any remedial problem, it is essential that your farrier work in consultation with your veterinarian.

studs

Metal studs are inserted into the heel of the shoe to give a better grip, especially when galloping or jumping. They are generally inserted only on the outside edge of the shoe, and are screwed into holes made by the farrier. Studs can be fitted and removed with a wrench. There are different studs for different conditions. Studs should be taken out when the horse is not working or when it is being ridden on the road (there are studs specially designed for road work), and the holes should be plugged to prevent them from filling with dirt.

above: *The hot-shoe method allows the farrier to get a close fit.*

the body of the horse

Conformation is the term used to explain the physical characteristics of a horse. The ideal varies depending on the breed and the work the horse is required to do. Proportion is all-important, because a correctly proportioned horse is better balanced and thus less prone to injury or unsoundness.

The general guidelines in assessing a horse's conformation are as follows:

The head well-set on and in proportion to the rest of its body, the eyes large, clear, and set well out at the side of the horse, and the ears medium-sized, pricked, and generally carried forward.

A muscular neck, with a correct proportion of length, well set into sloping, powerful shoulders, and the withers well-defined and of a reasonable height.

The limbs should be symmetrical and the horse should stand four-square, with the hind legs directly behind the forelegs. Each pair of legs should match, with joints the same size and both legs truly vertical. Seen from the side, the legs appear straight apart from the angle at the hock. The forelegs, when viewed from the front, should drop straight from the forearm to the foot, with sufficient bone immediately below the knee. The bone should be clean and flat and the tendons well defined. The forearm must be well-muscled and long, with the elbows clear of the body. The knees should be broad, flat and deep from the front to back, and the cannon bone short and straight; the fetlocks should be flat, while the pastern should be of medium length and sloping. The hind legs must be strong and well-formed; when viewed from the side, there should be plenty of length from stifle to hock, with a well-developed second thigh. The hocks should be

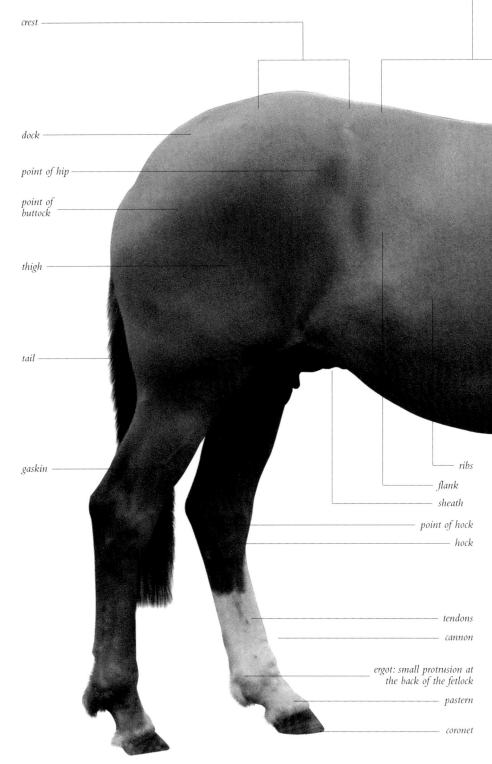

crest

dock

point of hip

point of buttock

thigh

tail

gaskin

ribs

flank

sheath

point of hock

hock

tendons

cannon

ergot: small protrusion at the back of the fetlock

pastern

coronet

back

neck

withers

crest

shoulder

mane

ears

poll

forelock

eye

cheek

projecting cheekbone

nostril

muzzle

chin groove

throat

windpipe

jugular groove

point of shoulder

breast

elbow

forearm

chestnut

knee

fetlock joint

heel

wall of hoof

large, with a well-defined look. The cannon bone below the hock should be short and strong.

The feet should neither turn in nor out, and there should be no swelling or puffiness around the joints and tendons. The heels should be wide, with a large, full frog capable of absorbing concussion and a slightly concave sole. The outside of the hoof, the wall, should have a smooth surface.

The depth of the body should be generous from just behind the withers to the lower line, just behind the elbows, with ribs that arch away from the backbone on either side to allow the lungs sufficient room for expansion. A generous chest allows room for a strong, healthy heart. A sufficient length of back is needed, especially if the horse is required for fast work, with short, muscular loins that are broad and deep. The hindquarters provide most of the power in the horse and should therefore be well-developed and muscular.

skeleton of the horse

The skeleton consists of around 210 bones and is made up of bone and cartilage. It is designed to provide support for the muscles and protection for the internal organs. Movement and locomotion are provided by the joints, ligaments, and muscles that hold the parts of the skeleton together.

The skeleton can be divided into two distinct parts: the axial and the appendenicular. The axial skeleton gives the body its shape and protects vital parts of the body. It is comprised of the skull, which protects the brain, and is large and elongated with three air-filled sinuses to reduce the weight; the backbone, which runs from the skull to the tail and carries and protects the spinal cord; and the rib-cage, which protects the heart, lungs, and other parts of the circulatory and digestive systems.

The appendicular skeleton consists of the shoulders and forelegs, the pelvic girdle, and hind legs. This part of the skeleton is supported by muscles and ligaments between the shoulders and by the pelvic girdle at the hindquarters, which is attached to the spine. As the forelegs take the larger portion of the horse's weight, their structure, from the shoulder-blade down, is specifically designed to absorb concussion. The construction of the hindquarters precipitates the production of quick and controlled power.

Bones are made up of a fibrous tissue known as collagen, together with the minerals calcium and phosphorous, and are covered by a membrane, called the periosteum, to which tendons and ligaments are attached. The ends of bones that form joints are covered in cartilage, a softer, tough substance that prevents friction, while sacs (bursae) that secrete synovial fluid (joint oil) encase the joints and act as a lubricant. Rigid bands of fibrous tissue, called ligaments, attach the bones on either side and support and regulate the movement of joints.

muscles

Muscles are made up of thousands of fibers that flex and extend to provide movement. They are arranged in overlapping bands and are controlled by nerves. Each muscle is attached to a stable part of the skeleton, while the other end is connected, sometimes by means of a tendon, to the part of the body or leg that is required to move. Most muscles work in pairs or groups; in order to facilitate movement, one muscle shortens (contracts) while the opposing muscle lengthens (relaxes), and vice versa. When not working, the muscles maintain the position of the skeletal frame and keep the horse in balance.

Tendons consist of collagen and are the cords that extend from the muscle and attach to the bones. Because of a relatively poor blood supply, tendons are slow to heal if damaged.

skin

The skin comprises of an outer layer (the epidermis) and an inner layer (the dermis). It is tough and elastic and varies in thickness, depending on which part of the body it is covering, but should always feel supple. The epidermis constantly replaces itself by producing new cells to replace the dead ones, while the dermis contains the nerve endings that detect pain, pressure, and heat.

The layer of fat beneath the skin, known as the subcutaneous fat, contains hair follicles and sweat glands, the latter secreting a substance known as sebum, which provides a waterproof layer for the coat.

The skin performs several functions:
• Protects the tissues below the surface from weather, infection, and minor injuries
• Acts as a sensory organ
• Stabilizes body heat by warming and cooling
• Absorb ultra-violet rays from sunlight. By synthesis, the body is able to make vitamin D from the sun's rays, which is absorbed through the skin, then into the blood

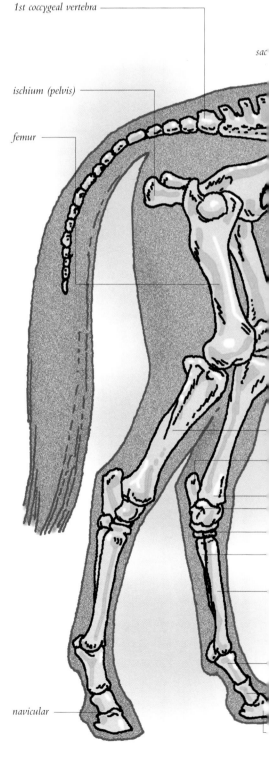

1st coccygeal vertebra

sac

ischium (pelvis)

femur

navicular

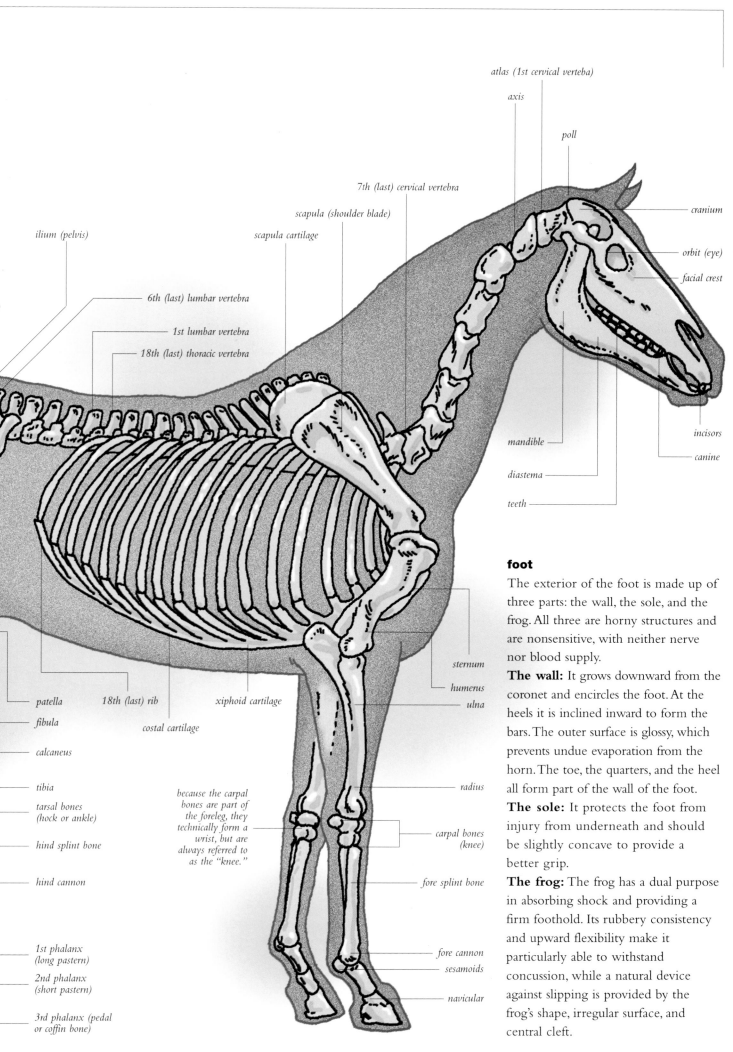

atlas (1st cervical verteba)

axis

poll

7th (last) cervical vertebra

scapula (shoulder blade)

scapula cartilage

ilium (pelvis)

cranium

orbit (eye)

facial crest

6th (last) lumbar vertebra

1st lumbar vertebra

18th (last) thoracic vertebra

mandible

incisors

canine

diastema

teeth

foot

The exterior of the foot is made up of three parts: the wall, the sole, and the frog. All three are horny structures and are nonsensitive, with neither nerve nor blood supply.

The wall: It grows downward from the coronet and encircles the foot. At the heels it is inclined inward to form the bars. The outer surface is glossy, which prevents undue evaporation from the horn. The toe, the quarters, and the heel all form part of the wall of the foot.

The sole: It protects the foot from injury from underneath and should be slightly concave to provide a better grip.

The frog: The frog has a dual purpose in absorbing shock and providing a firm foothold. Its rubbery consistency and upward flexibility make it particularly able to withstand concussion, while a natural device against slipping is provided by the frog's shape, irregular surface, and central cleft.

sternum

humerus

ulna

patella

18th (last) rib

xiphoid cartilage

fibula

costal cartilage

calcaneus

tibia

radius

tarsal bones (hock or ankle)

because the carpal bones are part of the foreleg, they technically form a wrist, but are always referred to as the "knee."

hind splint bone

carpal bones (knee)

hind cannon

fore splint bone

1st phalanx (long pastern)

fore cannon

sesamoids

2nd phalanx (short pastern)

navicular

3rd phalanx (pedal or coffin bone)

gaits of the horse

The horse possesses four natural gaits—walk, trot, canter, and gallop—although some breeds possess additional paces based on the ambling or pacing gait.

walk

The walk is a four-time pace, which means it has four beats to a stride. The steps should be even and regular. The usual sequence of footfalls is: left hind, left fore, right hind, right fore. The horse's hind foot should pass over the print left by the forefoot on the same side; this is called tracking up. The walk should be active and purposeful.

trot

The trot is a diagonal two-time pace, with two beats to the stride, the legs working in diagonal pairs. The sequence of footfalls should be: left hind and right fore, followed by right hind and left fore. The horse springs from one diagonal pair of legs to the other, with a brief moment when all four legs are off the ground. The pace should be rhythmic and active, without being hurried, to which the rider can rise or sit.

canter

The canter is a three-time pace, with three distinct beats and the legs working in diagonal pairs. The sequence of footfalls, when the left foreleg is leading, is: right hind, left hind and right fore together, left fore (the leading leg), with a moment when all four legs are briefly off the ground. The sequence when the right leg leads is: left hind, right hind and left fore together, right fore (the leading leg). The canter is probably the most comfortable pace and the rider should sit deep in the saddle.

gallop

The gallop is a four-time pace, with four rapid beats to each stride. As the horse increases its speed the tempo may be quickened and the stride lengthened, but the pace should remain rhythmic. The sequence of footfalls, with the left foreleg leading, should be: right hind, left hind, right fore, left fore, followed by a moment of suspension. The horse's outline lengthens and the rider should sit forward and slightly out of the saddle.

behavior of the horse

the horse as a herd animal

Horses are naturally herd animals and in the wild exist in groups comprising horses of both sexes and all ages. Horses prefer living in groups—in domestic situations these are generally single-sex—and a lone horse may pine or attempt to escape if its companions are removed.

While not naturally aggressive animals, fighting may occur in groups, generally triggered by an instinct to retain a position in the group's hierarchy. The horse's main defenses against any form of threat are its highly developed senses and its ability to retreat at speed. Since domestication, dangers—no longer wild animals but unexpected noises, movements, or sights—reawaken their instinct for flight. Alongside this, however, the horse retains its herd mentality, and it is unusual for a horse to refuse to pass by a strange object or noise if it sees others doing so safely.

equine senses

The horse has five highly developed senses, which contributed to the preservation of the species in the wild:

Sight: The horse's eyes are large and work independently of each other to cover a wide field of vision, with a small overlap at the center and a blind spot behind. The horse focuses on an object by raising or lowering its head, rather than altering the shape of the eye lens. The size of the eyes means that a horse can see well in the dark, although it is not nocturnal.

Hearing: The horse has an extremely acute sense of hearing, aided by the size and mobility of its ears, which rotate to register sounds from behind. Horses respond particularly well to being talked to; the human voice is one of the most valuable of all training tools.

Smell: In the wild, an acute sense of smell would have been used to detect desirable food. Horses appear to recognize their home by smell, borne out by the fact that they have a homing instinct. The action of throwing back the head and curling back the upper lip is known as flehmening, which is associated with sexual activity, as well as being a response to unusual smells or tastes.

Taste: Horses appear to like sweet and salty things, although they are also known to eat the more bitter varieties of herbs that grow in old pastures.

Touch: The horse has an acute sense of touch—it is one of the main forms of communication between horse and

below: *Horses communicate moods and emotions by using body language.*

left: *A horse's acute awareness of danger is sometimes referred to as its sixth sense.*

human, in the form of grooming. The whiskers on its muzzle are an important part of its sensory powers and allow a horse to sense nearby objects.

Horses reputedly have what we call a "sixth sense," often reacting to something that we are not aware of. Horses often are acutely aware of any impending danger.

body language

The horse uses its body to communicate a variety of moods and emotions. For example, if it has its ears back and is showing the whites of its eyes, it is displaying fear. If it is scared its instinct will be to retreat.

At rest, a horse stands with a hind leg resting with just one toe touching the ground, its ears are lower, its eyes half-closed, and its lower lip hangs down slightly. In the stable, the horse may turn its back to the door to indicate it does not want to be disturbed.

Impatience is normally indicated by stamping, shaking the head, or swishing the tail. Vocal communication includes neighing, squealing, and grunting, which can indicate pleasure, excitement, or aggression.

stable vices

Stable vices may occur in horses that are stabled for a large part of the day. Boredom can manifest itself in a number of ways, including repetitive behavior patterns such as crib-biting, when the horse fixes its jaw on a solid object, such as the top of the stable door or post, and arches its neck; box-walking, moving continuously around the stable; weaving, swinging the head from side to side; or wind-sucking, gulping in air.

below: *In the wild, horses live in groups comprising all ages and both sexes.*

health of the horse

Infectious diseases are caused by living organisms, most of which are so small that they cannot be seen by the naked eye. These are called micro-organisms and consist of viruses, bacteria, mycoplasma, chlamydia, rickettsia, and fungi. Infection can also be caused by protozoa and parasites; these are not as small as micro-organisms.

An infection means that a micro-organism has become established in the body's tissues, or on its surface, and reproduces itself to the detriment of the body. It damages or kills the animal's cells, which results in the symptoms of the disease developing. These are usually characteristic of the particular organism involved.

The organism causing an infectious disease must be identified to determine the correct treatment, future prognosis, and the relevance to horses that are stabled in the same yard.

causes of disease

Bacteria
Bacteria are usually single-celled organisms that are found living in soil and water or within a host—a plant or an animal. In healthy animals, bacteria live on the skin, in the mouth, around the teeth, in the upper respiratory tract, in genitalia, and occur in large numbers in the gut, where they help to break down food.

Bacterial infections usually arise when organisms gain access to sensitive tissue within the body via inhalation, ingestion, or through breaks in the skin, for example wounds. Some infections can exert their effects by overwhelming the normal flora of the horse (in the gut, for example). When they enter the horse and find a suitable site, they multiply and produce toxins, which in turn cause the clinical symptoms that characterize the particular disease.

Viruses
Viruses are sub-microscopic organisms and can only be seen with the aid of an electron microscope. They usually cause specific diseases such as influenza. Diagnosis of a viral disease is difficult, since an undetected virus may occur before a bacterial infection such as a cough or nasal discharge is noticed, although the infection is a direct result of the virus. Alternatively, there may be evidence of the presence of a virus at a time when the horse is exhibiting no symptoms.

Mycoplasma, rickettsia, and chlamydia
Next to viruses, mycoplasma are the smallest free-living organisms and can cause diseases in animals. Rickettsia are only associated with infections spread by lice, fleas, ticks, and mites. Chlamydia cause diseases in man and other animals.

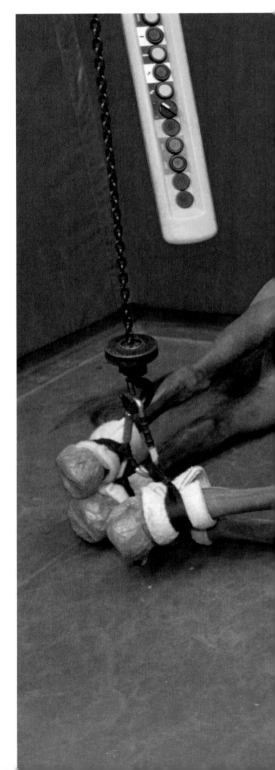

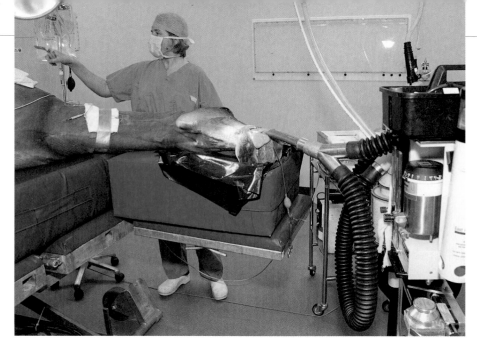

left and below: *Theater workings. A horse is prepared for surgery (left) and afterward is restrained and protected during the recovery period.*

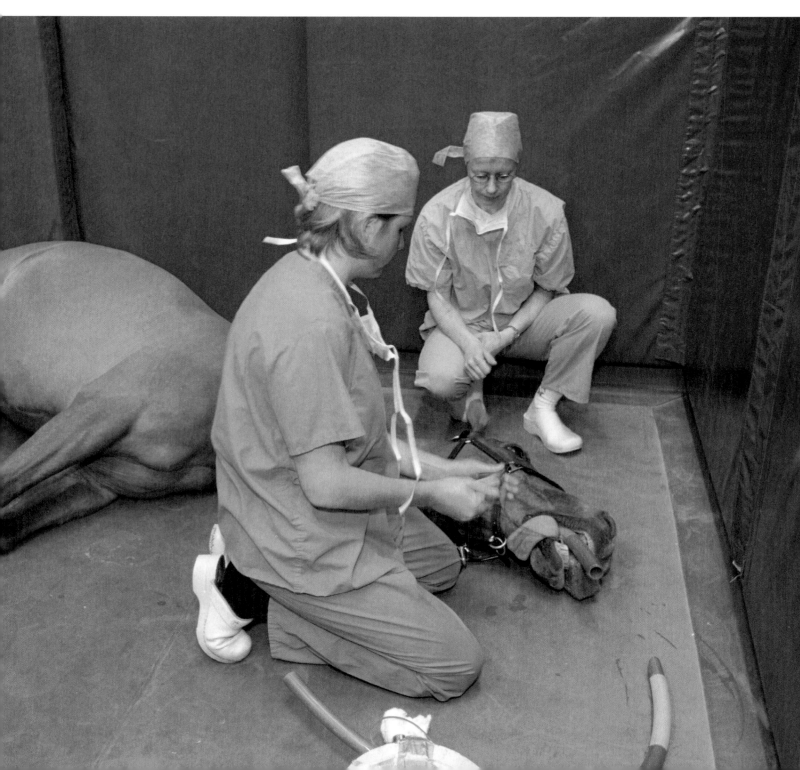

Fungi

Fungi are larger than bacteria. They mainly live in the soil or on plants and reproduce themselves via spores. These spores can cause an allergic reaction in horses without causing an infection. Fungal spores enter the tissues of the horse and germinate and create a seat of infection. The most common fungal infections in the horse are surface skin infections and ringworm.

Parasites

A parasite lives in or on its host, from which it obtains nourishment. It can damage the tissues of the host to cause disease. Parasites can be joint-limbed (for example, lice and ticks), worms, or protozoa.

Worms such as roundworms or tapeworms can be transferred from horse to horse without the intervention of another organism. They may exist for a time as a free-living stage outside the host, for example in the pasture, before being transferred to another horse.

Having had a parasitic infection, horses may be able to kill all or some of the parasites invading in a second or later infection. This is the protective immune response and explains why older horses tend to be less susceptible to infection than foals or youngsters.

diseases of the joints

JOINT ILL
Symptoms

Warm, painful, swollen joint. Seen in foals, but occasionally in an adult horse. Animals are often depressed and off food with a high temperature.

Cause

Infection originating from the blood in foals via the navel, especially if they have received insufficient colostrum. In the adult horse, it usually occurs as a sequel to a wound.

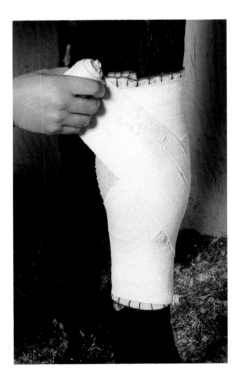

OSTEOARTHRITIS
Symptoms

Lameness may vary from mild to severe and may be sudden or gradual in onset. Affected joints are not always swollen. Bone spavin in the hock and ringbone in the pastern joints are common examples.

Cause

Abnormal stresses on a joint, often due to poor conformation and leading to the degeneration of the joint cartilage resulting in bone change. It can also occur after a direct traumatic injury.

diseases of the legs, nerves, and muscles

TENDON STRAIN
Symptoms

Mild to severe lameness with heat, swelling, and pain behind the cannon bone. More often found in the forelegs than the hind legs.

Cause

Uneven or abnormal stresses on the tendon, especially when the horse is tiring and moving at speed or jumping. Back-at-the-knee conformation and hyper-extended fetlock joints with long sloping pasterns predispose to injury.

AZOTURIA
Symptoms

Mild cases exhibit stiffness that may be transient and associated with gait changes. In severe cases the horse is reluctant or unable to move, with muscle stiffness and spasms, usually seen in the back or hindquarter muscles. Urine may be red or brown.

Cause

Occurs during severe exercise after the horse has been rested for a day or more without cutting back on hard feed. Sometimes seen after extreme exertion.

TETANUS
Symptoms

This is characterized by a reluctance to move, restricted jaw movement, and often an anxious and alert expression. The horse may have a raised tail and prolapse of the third eyelid. This can progress to more severe muscle stiffness, collapse, and death.

Cause

Infection by *Clostridium tetani*, a bacterium found in the soil. It enters the body via wounds, surgical procedures, and through mucosal ulceration.

below: *Hosing down a wound removes any dirt and helps to reduce swelling.*

right: *A gray mare with laminitis—a painful inflamation of the sensitive area of the laminae (membranes) that are located between the horny wall of the horse's hoof and pedal bone.*

diseases of the foot

NAIL BIND OR PRICK
Symptoms
Mild to moderately severe lameness with pain reflex shown when the offending nail is pressurized. Usually occurs within a few days of shoeing (bind) or sooner (prick).
Cause
The shoe nail has been applied too close to the sensitive white line of the hoof (bind) or into the sensitive tissues of the foot (prick).

PUS IN THE FOOT
Symptoms
Slight to severe lameness that may vary from day to day. Often the affected leg fills to the fetlock joint and above. The foot feels warm and the digital blood vessels have a bounding pulse. It is the most common cause of lameness in horses.
Cause
Infection following puncture wounds or as a sequel to cracks in the white line. Anaerobic bacteria (ones needing little or no oxygen) are often involved.

LAMINITIS
Symptoms
Characterized by a reluctance to move and the transfer of weight onto the back heels of the foot. The forefeet are often held out in front, with the hind feet placed well underneath the body. The feet are usually warm, with bounding digital pulses.
Cause
Classically seen in overweight ponies irregularly exercised, especially when the grass is growing rapidly. It may occur after a horse or pony eats excessive quantities of carbohydrate (grain overload), with generalized toxemia such as after diarrhea. It can also occur in the opposite leg to a lame one, because the horse bears too much weight on the unaffected limb. Laminitis can be triggered by excessive work on hard ground, too.

CORNS
Symptoms
Produces mild and often intermittent lameness. It is more obvious when the horse turns and the affected foot is on the inside.
Cause
Bruising between the wall and the bars of the foot. Horses with flat feet and thin soles are more susceptible. It can be the result of standing on a solid object such as a stone or of excessive work on hard ground.

THRUSH
Symptoms
An infection of the frog. The horn of the frog is black, moist, and putrid. There may be no lameness.
Cause
It is due to poor hygiene and a failure to clean out the feet regularly, or from allowing the horse to stand in dirty, moist conditions. Horses with long toes are more prone to the condition.

OVERREACH
Symptoms
This is the bruising and laceration of the heels or coronary band of a forelimb, often resulting in severe lameness relative to the extent of the wound.
Cause
The horse has struck into himself with the toe of his hind foot.

right: *In sporting events, the health of the competing horse is paramount. Here, a vet conducts a compulsory stop check during an event at Cirencester Park, England.*

NAVICULAR DISEASE

Symptoms

The horse initially shows a shortening of its stride and becomes uneven on turns, particularly on hard ground. May "point" one or both toes when standing at rest. The situation progresses to mild lameness, often with excessive wear of the toes leading to frequent stumbling.

Cause

Not yet fully understood. It is exclusively seen in the front feet of horses. Ponies are rarely affected.

diseases of the skin

RINGWORM

Symptoms

Characterized by small rounded patches of hair loss that gradually increase in size with scab formation. The head, neck, base of tail, and girth areas are most commonly involved.

Causes

By fungi, most commonly *Trichophyton* and *microsporum* species, through direct contact with infected horses, and indirectly by shared tack, brushes, and stables.

MUD FEVER

(Cutaneous streptothricosis)

Symptoms

Characterized by oozing and scab formation, often with loss of hair. Not an irritant but can be extremely sensitive to the touch and results in lameness when affecting the fetlock, pastern, and bulb of the heel.

Cause

An infection with a bacterium called *Dermatophilus congolensis*. Prolonged wet weather predisposes to the condition, as the damp, muddy hair and skin on the horse's legs has no opportunity to dry.

SWEET ITCH

Symptoms

The scaling and crusting of the skin that usually affects the withers, mane, tail, and head. The horse rubs the affected areas because they are irritable; the skin thickens and wrinkles with repeated episodes.

Cause

A seasonal allergic reaction of the skin to the saliva of biting midges, *Culicoides* species. It can affect all types of horses. Ponies are particularly prone to the condition.

SARCOIDS

Symptoms

Common skin tumor that may be verrucous (dry and often cauliflower-like in appearance) or fibroblastic (with hard fibrous nodules), or a mixture of both.

Cause

As yet unknown.

diseases of the digestive system

CHOKE

Symptoms

The horse is usually very uncomfortable, with its head and neck extended. Saliva and food material pour from the nostrils. The horse may be coughing and trying to swallow repeatedly, as if trying to clear its throat.

Cause

Obstruction of the esophagus by impacted food. The most common culprit is sugar beet pulp or sugar beet nuts that have been inadequately soaked. It is more common in tired horses or ones that bolt their food.

QUIDDING

Symptoms

The horse drops its food, particularly chewed forage, from the mouth.

Cause

This is due to the development of sharp points on the outside of the upper teeth and on the inside of the lower teeth. Sharp points or hooks can also develop on the first upper cheek tooth and on the last lower cheek tooth on each side.

COLIC

Symptoms

This is the name given to abdominal pain. Symptoms include restlessness, sweating, pawing the ground, kicking or looking around at the abdomen, rolling, lying on the ground, or constantly getting up and down. The horse is unlikely to eat or drink.

Cause

It may be spasmodic, which is usually transient, relapsing, and self-limiting; tympanitic due to gas distention of the stomach or intestine; or impactive. The latter arises from the obstruction of the large intestine, most commonly the large colon, by hard, dry food material. Colic can also be caused by an obstruction of the intestine, resulting in lessening of the blood flow in the gut wall or compromised nerve impulses. Many horses who experience colic have a history of worm damage to the gut wall or to intestinal blood vessels.

DIARRHEA

Symptoms

This may be chronic or acute, depending on the cause. The affected horse may otherwise seem well and lose weight gradually, or it may be severely ill with dullness, weakness, fever, dehydration, and often abdominal pain.

below: *Taking the horse's temperature will help to establish its condition.*

Cause

There are many different causes, which vary in severity and outcome. These include overfeeding with high protein foodstuffs; bacterial, e.g. *salmonella*; viral, e.g., rotavirus in foals; parasitic, e.g., redworms; tumors and poisoning, e.g., molds.

diseases of the respiratory tract

STRANGLES

Symptoms

Signs include depression, loss of appetite, fever with a slight cough, clear or later yellowish nasal discharge, and lymph node enlargement.

Cause

The bacterium *Streptococcus equi*, which is highly infectious.

VIRAL RESPIRATORY DISEASE

Symptoms

Symptoms vary but include coughing, discharge from both nostrils, fever, painful or enlarged lymph nodes, depression, dullness, poor appetite, and poor performance.

Cause

Many different types of viruses have been implicated, including equine influenza and the herpes viruses.

C.O.P.D or STABLE COUGH

Symptoms

Most cases are mild but it can occasionally present itself as an acute asthmatic-like attack. Clinical signs are intermittent, depending on exposure

above: *Sweet itch is a seasonal allergic reaction to midges and generally affects the mane, tail, withers, and head areas.*

to the causative allergens. The cough is often more noticeable at night or when the horse begins to trot during exercise. The respiratory rate is increased and in chronic or severe cases there is a double expiratory movement. This is marked by a "heave" line caused by increased use of muscles in the lower abdomen.

Cause

This is the most common cause of chronic respiratory disease in adult horses and is due to an allergy to inhaled spores of molds. The condition is exacerbated by the dust often associated with hay and straw. The allergy usually develops gradually but may be triggered acutely.

LUNGWORM

Symptoms

Characterized by a persistent cough for many months, especially in late summer and autumn. The coughing is often in severe bouts, with the head lowered close to the ground.

Cause

This is usually seen in mature horses and is due to the parasite *Dictyocaulus arnfieldii*. The likely source of infection is sharing pasture with or after donkeys, who have a much higher incidence of infection.

alternative therapies

Complementary therapies such as herbalism, homeopathy, acupuncture, and massage have their roots in ancient traditions, but in more recent years these forms of alternative treatment have come to the attention of horse owners, many of whom are turning to them in preference to—or in conjunction with—chemical medicines.

herbalism

The knowledge and use of herbs is thousands of years old—herbs as medicines were prescribed as far back as ancient Egyptian times. Herbalism involves the use of natural sources to supply the required minerals and vitamins vital to maintain health.

The aim of herbalism is to prevent rather than cure, and the use of these plants is therefore directed at promoting the total health of the horse. Through the ages, herbs have been prescribed for many different purposes, including as a relaxant, a tonic, to calm nerves, ease pain, and reduce fevers. One herb, alfalfa, which contains an

right: *Modern technology can be beneficial to any muscle complaints your horse may have. As with humans, a course of ultrasound treatment can be just the tonic.*

excellent source of essential vitamins and minerals, is also used as a feed, either as a concentrate, in the form of pellets, or as a source of roughage.

homeopathy

In orthodox medicine the theory is that the symptoms of a condition need to be treated. In homeopathy the idea is that the symptoms are a response of the body's defense systems to an invasion and that these symptoms should be stimulated rather than suppressed.

While homeopathy, like herbalism, relies on ingredients derived from natural sources, unlike herbalism there is no standard remedy for a known condition; each case is assessed individually and a specific remedy detailed. A treatment analysis is based not only on the symptoms experienced, but also on the character of the individual, as well as the environment. A number of homeopathic remedies are available for use in first aid, such as arnica, which comes in tablet form or as a lotion or cream and is used to prevent bruising, and witch hazel, which can help reduce bleeding.

acupuncture and acupressure

Traditional Chinese medicine is part of a complex philosophy that remains alien to many Western cultures. Acupuncture and acupressure, while often wrongly thought of as single therapies, are two parts of this whole approach. In its simplest terms, the aim of Chinese medicine is to achieve overall balance and help prevent

left: *Massage is becoming more widely employed as an alternative therapy for equines.*

sickness by considering the whole and not just the symptoms. In acupuncture, fine needles are inserted beneath the skin at selected points, whereas in acupressure certain points are stimulated by the use of small metal balls or finger pressure.

massage

Massage is a widely used therapy for humans and can be applied to similar effect on equines. While it requires a knowledge of the structure of muscles, different types, and the role each one plays in the movement of the horse, it is less complex than the therapies previously discussed. Massage involves rubbing parts of the horse's body, which affects the muscle structures within.

A masseur can employ a number of different strokes. These include effleurage, a technique involving the use of both hands, which are molded over the body contours with contact via the palm of the hand, thumb, and

fingers; kneading, a single-handed technique using the hand clenched in a loose fist, with the backs of the fingers and the knuckles positioned over the relevant area; wringing, a double-handed technique where the skin and underlying tissue are picked up within the palm and fingers of first one hand, then the other; and skin rolling, where a flap of skin is picked up between fingers and thumbs then pushed away using thumb pressure against the fingers. In this way, as the hands move away from the body, one area of skin "rolls" into another.

While many individuals and organizations promote the use and benefit of alternative therapies, these forms of treatment attract their fair share of critics. It is wise, therefore, that you seek expert advice from both camps so as to be fully aware of the pros and cons of any method of treatment you intend to use.

learning to ride

starting off

Whenever you decide to learn to ride, the first few steps are likely to be the same. You need to find a safe place to learn and an instructor in whom you have confidence and to whom you can relate. Both requirements will normally be fulfilled by an established riding school or equestrian center.

The best way of finding such an establishment in the United States is to contact the American Riding Instructors' Association (in New Hampshire), which has a directory of certified riding schools, or the Certified Horsemanship Association (in Texas). Young riders can contact the local branch of the U.S. Pony Club. In the UK, contact the British Horse Society or the Association of British Riding Schools. Otherwise, personal

recommendation by a person experienced in horses or a glance through advertisements in equestrian magazines may yield results.

choosing a school

While in most cases your choice will be limited to schools in your area, some people think it is worthwhile to travel a long distance to attend a recommended school. Wherever you decide to ride, always visit the school prior to arranging lessons and, if possible, visit more than one school, in order to compare different styles of teaching. If possible, take along an experienced person, particularly if you are looking for a riding school for a child and have little equestrian knowledge yourself.

Some basic points to look out for when visiting a riding center

1. Is the stable yard tidy and well kept?
2. Are the staff friendly and helpful?
3. Are the horses and ponies happy and healthy-looking?
4. Is the tack and equipment clean and well maintained?
5. Are the stables and fields well kept, with safe fencing?
6. Do the pupils look like they are having fun and enjoying their lessons?

Other points to consider

1. If relevant to your needs, does the school cater to people with disabilities?
2. What facilities does it have? Does it have indoor and/or outdoor arenas? Does it have a cross-country course?
3. What sort of hacking is there around the school? Is there plenty of off-road riding?
4. Are there a number of instructors?
5. Does the school offer private lessons?
6. Does it offer lessons in different disciplines? (This point may not be relevant to begin with, but may become so when you are more experienced.)

left: *Hacking offers a relaxing and enjoyable complement to more formal instruction.*

right: *A riding hat made to the highest current safety standards is an essential piece of equipment when you start riding.*

below: *Before choosing a riding school it is helpful to sit in on a lesson to see how a class is taught.*

Sit in on a lesson, if you are permitted to do so. Note how many people there are in the class and whether there is more than one lesson going on in the same arena. Observe how the instructor relates to the pupils and how interesting he/she makes the lesson. Are all the riders participating in the lesson, or are some doing very little while one or two receive most of the attention?

basic equipment

The most important piece of equipment to purchase when you start riding is a riding hat or jockey skull made to the highest current safety standards. Although most riding schools provide hats, it is better to have your own fitted by an expert.

Riding boots are not a prerequisite, but do not wear shoes or boots with ridged soles, as your foot may get stuck in the stirrups. Leggings (without an inside seam) may be worn and will be more comfortable than jeans, which rub. An approved make of body protector is something you may wish to purchase when you progress to faster work and jumping, although children often wear one right from the start.

the first lesson

If possible, arrange your first few lessons on a one-to-one basis. Your instructor should provide you with a suitable horse, in terms of size and temperament, and you will probably be led on a lead rein or a lunge rein, where the instructor controls the horse from the center of the arena on a long rein. Riding on a lunge allows the inexperienced rider to concentrate on his/her position and enables the horse to move more freely, though still under the instructor's control.

The first things your teacher will tell you is how to get on the horse; how to hold the reins; and the correct seat (riding position). You will also learn to remain balanced at the three paces of walk, trot, and canter. From the outset, keep looking toward where you wish to go, not at the horse's hooves. Try to relax and remember, above all, that riding is meant to be enjoyable. Don't be afraid to ask questions—if you are unhappy about something or don't understand what you are being told, tell your

instructor. As you progress, you can ask to lead the horse in and tack and untack it. Talk to your horse all the time—this may seem strange at first, but everyone does it!

When you first start riding, or if you ride again after a long period out of the saddle, you may find that you are very stiff afterward. This is natural and your body will soon become accustomed to using the muscles exercised while riding. Other physical activities, like swimming and cycling, can help to make you more supple.

as you progress

Once you have mastered the basics of walk, trot, and canter, you may find it more fun to join a group lesson. Your instructor will place you in a class with people at your level of ability. One thing you will quickly realize is that you never stop learning, and that even very experienced riders benefit from lessons.

On the perimeter of the school arena you will see the markers A, K, E, H, C, M, B, F. You will use these when riding circles, serpentines, and other figures that help to improve your control of the horse. When you feel fairly confident—and when your instructor feels it is safe for you to do so—you can go out on hacks. This type of riding increases your confidence, but be sure that it is at a level with which you feel happy. If you don't feel in control, you can always ask to slow to a walk and simply enjoy the scenery and the pleasure of being outside on horseback.

left: *Jumping reinforces the rider's skills of balance and coordination.*

above: *Riding figure shapes such as circles and serpentines all help to improve your control of the horse.*

Once you have reached a certain standard in your flat work, you will be taught to jump. Although some may not wish to pursue this activity as far as others, the basics of jumping are helpful in reinforcing the rider's skills, particularly those of balance and coordination. Jumping lessons usually start with the use of trotting poles placed on the ground and very tiny fences in a grid, set for your horse's stride. Eventually you will build up to jumping a course of fences.

One you have established the basics of riding, you can progress in many different directions. You may find that you are a weekend rider who enjoys hacking out, or alternatively you may choose to concentrate on a specific discipline, such as jumping or dressage. You may even want to buy your own horse. However you progress, you will find that riding is one of the greatest pleasures in life.

training the young horse

Training or producing a young horse is one of the most satisfying ways of developing your horsemanship, but it is not a realistic option for the inexperienced rider. Only after working with a number of different types of horses will a competent rider be able to anticipate situations and have gained sufficient insight into the equine mind.

If you are determined to train your own horse, whether a foal or an unbroken three-year-old, it is probably worth engaging the help of a more experienced trainer. It is also worth considering whether you have the correct facilities at home. These should include an enclosed indoor and outdoor arena and help from people on the ground, when necessary. Once backed, young horses initially need to be ridden every day and riders must be committed to the task. You will have to display patience, tact, firmness, and consistency.

early lessons

Training begins when the foal is only a few days old. Foals spend most of their time in the field with their dams and will accept wearing a lightweight head collar when they see that it holds no fear for others. Foals do not need to be over-handled but, if they become confident with people from an early age, they will be easier to manage when serious work begins. In the meantime, insist on good manners from the start and gradually introduce grooming and picking out of feet. The latter will help at the farrier's first visit.

When handling a foal, massage the top of the gums and look at the teeth. This will help introduce the idea of having a bit in its mouth. A regular worming program should be carried out in the first few years. When necessary, foals and youngsters should be given hard food to help them reach their full growing potential. They should also be checked over daily, as a permanent blemish may occur if a cut or wound is not treated and stitched immediately.

training methods

Starting a horse or breaking it in for riding usually begins when it is three years old. As the horse is not yet fully mature, this makes the process easier. However, once the horse is confident being ridden out alone and in company, it should be turned away again and left to develop both physically and mentally.

Riding a horse for the first time should be tackled gradually. Although this usually takes about six weeks, the method of join-up, pioneered by (among others) the American Monty Roberts, has gained a considerable

right: *A happy, well behaved, and willing horse is the ultimate aim in training a youngster.*

above: *This horse is wearing a lunge cavesson.*

following worldwide and may take as little as 30 minutes. Roberts' theory is based on the assumption that whatever action the horse makes, it is most likely to be influenced by you. This is especially true of the young, unstarted horse. Roberts' aim is to create a relationship based on trust and confidence, where the horse wants to join-up with his partner on the ground and accept the saddle, bridle, and rider with no trauma.

After a few days spent getting the horse used to the bit, and a small measure of communication (through long lines and his mouth), the horse will be ready to join-up. The ideal environment for this is a 50-foot (15.25-m) diameter round pen with a good surface. The trainer works quietly with the horse, mimicking the dominant mare in a herd by repeatedly chasing the youngster away. Gradually the young horse realizes that the most pleasant place to be is with the trainer, waiting for instruction.

After joining-up with the horse, the Monty Roberts method advises using your hands to massage the neck, withers, back, hips, and flanks on both sides, after which the horse

should be ready to have each of its feet picked up. The saddle pad, saddle, and bridle are introduced, then the rider is ready to mount. The horse is ridden in circles at a walk and trot. The aim of this process is that the horse elects to stay with the trainer rather than go away. The procedure is carried out without restriction to the animal.

Much of the success of the join-up process is based on watching the horse's body language. This may take some time to learn and it should not be carried out by unskilled trainers. Instead, if you wish to carry out Monty Roberts' methods, practice with an older, more reliable horse first and never take unnecessary risks.

further training

By a more conventional method, the unbroken horse is lunged. This means that the trainer controls the horse from the ground, working in a circle. The trainer can also follow the horse from behind, controlling it with long reins that run along either side (or both sides) of its body.

Once the horse is working freely, a roller (a broad strap that goes around the body and is normally used to hold a rug in place) is introduced. This is gradually tightened over the next few

days to accustom the horse to wearing a girth. A bridle is then added, either with a plain rubber snaffle or a mouthing bit. The latter has dangling keys that sit on the tongue and encourage the horse to chew.

Before introducing a saddle, the horse is allowed a long look at it. It is important to ensure that, when the saddle is put on the horse's back, the girth is tight enough for it not to slip under the animal's belly. It is now time for the horse to take a little weight on its back. To achieve this, the rider leans halfway up the saddle and a helper takes most of the rider's weight. Every day the rider puts a little more weight on the saddle until he/she is leaning across it from both sides.

When the horse is happy with the weight, a few steps can be introduced. Then the rider begins to make some movements himself, still leaning over the saddle. An agile rider is needed to finally move into the saddle. The rider remains lying along the horse's neck and sits slightly higher in the saddle each day.

riding the young horse

The rider should talk to and reassure the horse all the time. Very gently and slowly, the rider introduces leg and rein aids. Gradually, the helper on the floor gives fewer instructions and the rider in the saddle gives more. At this stage it is important for the rider to sit quietly and calmly and give clear commands. Work sessions should be kept short, since young horses cannot concentrate for long periods. Once the horse can walk, trot, and canter calmly in the school, it is time for it to be ridden out with a schoolmaster—an older, experienced horse.

Venturing only a little way from home to start with, the younger and older horses take turns leading. The periods away from home are increased daily. If the youngster is worried by anything at any point, the schoolmaster is close behind to give a lead before the obstacle becomes an issue. When the young horse is confident riding out with a lead, it's time for it to be ridden out alone. When the youngster is finally going forward freely, both in the school and on a hack, it is turned out for a well-earned rest.

Once the horse is four years old, it may be introduced to poles on the ground, leading up to small grids of jumps and, eventually, courses. It is important that the horse be ridden correctly at this stage, so that it learns to work from behind and come on to the bit. All lessons should be as varied as possible, in order to maintain interest.

Training a young horse is rarely straightforward, but it is important to remain calm and treat every horse as an individual. If you hit a problem, go back a stage or two to rebuild the horse's confidence before moving on again. Try to avoid conflict: Instead of forcing your horse to do something, try to encourage it to do so because it wants to. Your ultimate goal in training a youngster is to end up with a well-behaved, happy, and willing horse.

below: *Handling a foal sensitively from the beginning will help it gain confidence and thus make formal training more effective.*

buying a horse

Buying a horse is a huge commitment that is guaranteed to change your lifestyle, in terms of both time and money. At the very least, a horse turned out at grass needs visiting once a day and feeding throughout the winter. Stable-kept horses not only need exercising, but also have to be fed three or four times a day and need checking last thing at night. However, once you have made the decision to buy a horse and have found facilities where it may be kept, either on your premises or at a boarding stable, the next step is to find your ideal animal.

Viewing horses for sale is a time-consuming business, so first realistically appraise your aspirations, riding ability, and experience. Do you have ambitions to go show jumping or eventing, or are you a weekend rider, happy to hack and school your horse from home? Depending on what you want to do, the type of horse you should choose varies considerably, and so does the price.

Contact anyone you already know and trust in the equestrian world who may either have, or know of, horses of the right type that are for sale. Do not be afraid to visit a reputable dealer for, unlike a private owner, he has a reputation to maintain. It is also worth

scouring the "horses for sale" section in the equestrian press and in local newspapers, or placing an advertisement yourself under the "horses wanted" category. Horses are often purchased from horse sales, but this option is for professionals only, not the first-time buyer.

choosing the correct type

When answering an advertisement, try to find out as much as possible about the horse for sale, as it could save you a wasted trip. In general, never consider a pony that is not 100 percent traffic-proof for a child, or one that is too young and "green" for an inexperienced rider. If an owner claims that a pony has attended Pony Club rallies, find out which branch they belong to and call the district

right: *If possible, watch the horse being tacked up and note whether it is easy to handle.*

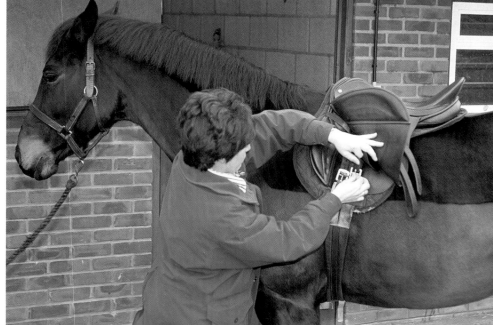

commissioner, who should be able to tell you something about the pony.

The type of horse is also important, since there is little point in putting a heavyset man on a lightweight Thoroughbred. Temperament is crucial: the horse will become a member of your family, and few people welcome a bad-tempered individual with an unenthusiastic outlook on life. Unfortunately, it is wise to be suspicious of anyone selling horses, since all of them will have some faults. The secret is to discover whether they are faults you can live with or not.

Owning a horse that is difficult to shoe causes problems, as does owning one that is difficult to box. However, neither of these problems is insurmountable, and may, with time and patience, be overcome. Bad conformation, a difficult temperament, and established stable habits, such as wind-sucking, prove more challenging—horses displaying any of these are best avoided. If you do not get along with your horse for any reason, selling him later will be easier if you avoid fundamental problems. Some people state a preference for geldings, because they are reputedly less

above: *When viewing a horse, assess its conformation and type before asking to see it being ridden.*

temperamental than mares, so it is worth bearing this in mind.

First stand back and take a long, hard look at the animal. The head should be well set onto a well-formed neck. A horse with a short, stocky neck is more difficult to "get on the bridle." A good, sloping shoulder suggests a free mover, while a short-backed horse is easier to ride than a long-backed one with poorly made hocks.

view at all paces

The conformation of the front legs is important and the cannon bone/tendon length ratio should not be too long and should be consistent with the rest of the leg. The pastern should be set at an angle of about 45 degrees, as should the foot, which must be a good shape. A horse's feet should be neither too flat nor too boxy, nor should they resemble long, donkey-shaped feet that have little shock-absorbing ability.

Once you have assessed a horse's type and conformation, watch it walk and trot up in hand. Note whether it moves "straight" or not. At the walk, it should overtrack its fore feet with its hind ones. You can see this by noting where its front foot hits the

below: *It is wise to see the horse being ridden first before trying it yourself.*

ground then seeing how close to this spot the back foot falls. A good walker is invariably a good galloper. Now see the horse trot in hand and watch for elevation in its stride and the engagement of its hindquarters.

If you are still interested, ask to see the horse ridden, so that you can see it canter. Unless you are an experienced rider, it is unwise to sit on an unknown horse without seeing it ridden first. At the canter you are looking for an athletic, elevated stride that covers the ground. Throughout this process, you should note the horse's temperament and its attitude toward work.

Do not ride the horse unless you are interested in buying it, as it is a waste of everyone's time. However, once on board, make sure your assessment from the ground was correct. Does it feel comfortable, will you enjoy riding it, and is it easy and willing to ride? Try it at all paces, in circles and coming back

to the halt, and walk often, to determine how well schooled it is and how strong it is in the mouth.

trust the vet's judgment

The next step is to see it jump. Here the horse's attitude is more important than its potential jumping ability. If possible, see it over a cross-country fence or a "spooky" show jump, as this tells you more about its personality and its degree of boldness. Style is also important, and a more experienced horse who dangles its front legs will not be the safest conveyance. However, this is less significant in a youngster, as it may not yet have learned to fold its front legs.

The most important factor is your gut feeling as a rider: Do you want to jump the horse and can you imagine yourselves as happy partners? Ride it back to the stable yard and then past it, to test whether it is nappy or not. If

above: *The vetting procedure includes a thorough manual examination of the horse.*

it resists at this stage and wants to go home, it is not the one to buy.

If you decide it is the horse for you, always have your own veterinarian (not the vendor's) examine it before you purchase. Inform the vet of what you hope to do with the horse and the amount of money you are paying for it. The vet can establish that the horse is sound, has no old scars or injuries that may cause problems in the future, and check its eyes, wind, and heart. Disappointing as it may be, if your vet considers the horse unsuitable, it is wise not to go ahead. And remember, although some problems may invariably raise their heads during the course of ownership, it is important never to buy a problem.

glossary

ABRS Association of British Riding Schools.

Acupuncture A form of Chinese medicine where fine needles are used to stimulate pressure points.

Action The way in which the horse moves its legs at each pace.

African Horse Sickness A seasonal viral disease.

AHS Arab Horse Society.

Aids Signals made by the rider to communicate instructions to the horse. Artificial aids are the whip and spurs; natural aids are the legs, hands, bodyweight, and voice.

Arena polo A version of the traditional game played on all-weather surfaces with three members per team.

Back (at the knee) The lower part of the leg, below the knee, curves back.

Back (hollow) The natural concave line of the horse's back is exaggerated.

Balance When a horse moves correctly, it balances itself against the weight of the rider.

Ballotade A movement in *haute ecole* where the horse jumps forward off the ground from a half-rearing position and lands on all four legs.

Bandages Used on the legs for protection, support, and warmth, and on the tail to prevent rubbing and keep the hairs flat.

Bar shoe A remedial shoe with bars connecting at the heels to give additional support.

Barrel The part of the body between the forearms and loins.

Bars (a) The gum between the molars and incisors where the bit rests; (b) the ends of the hoof wall, from the end of the wall to the sole.

BDS British Driving Society.

Beagles Foot packs used to hunt hares.

BHS British Horse Society

Bloodstock Thoroughbred horses that are bred for racing.

Blue feet Dense, blue-black horn.

Boarding stable Privately owned horses are kept and looked after at a yard for a prearranged fee.

Boaters Canal horses of the eighteenth century

Body brush A short-bristled brush used to remove grease and condition the coat of a stabled horse.

Bone The measurement of bone measured just below the knee, or hock, determines the horse's weight-carrying ability.

Breaking The initial education of a horse for whatever purpose is intended.

Bridle The headpiece that connects the bit and the reins.

Bridoon A type of snaffle that is used with a curb bit and chain in a double bridle.

Broodmare A mare used for breeding purposes.

Browband The piece of the bridle that sits across the horse's forehead, below its ears.

BSJA British Show Jumping Association.

Calf roping One of the five standard events in a rodeo.

Cannon bone The bone between the knee and fetlock of the foreleg.

Canter A three-time pace.

Cantle The raised part at the back of the saddle.

Capriole A movement in *haute ecole* where the horse leaps forward from a half-rearing position, kicking out with its hind legs.

Cast (a shoe) When a shoe comes off by accident

Cast (in stable) A horse that is lying down and cannot get up, usually one that has rolled over too close to the wall.

Cavesson A type of noseband that fits underneath the cheekpieces.

Cheekpiece (a) Part of the bridle that attaches the bit at one end and the headpiece at the other; (b) the straight side-bits on some bits.

Chukka A period of play in a game of polo.

Classics The five main English Flat races for three-year-olds: the Derby, the Oaks, the St. Leger, the 1000 Guineas, and 2000 Guineas.

Clench The part of the nail used in shoeing that comes out from the wall of the hoof and is bent over and hammered in to secure the shoe.

Cob A short-legged, stocky horse, capable of carrying substantial weight.

Colic Abdominal pain caused by the distention of the gut due to a build-up of gas, overeating, or a blockage.

Competition horse Horse specifically bred to compete in one of the four main equestrian disciplines of showjumping, eventing, dressage, and carriage driving.

Compound feeds A complete balanced feed available in different grades, either as a coarse mix or in cube form.

Concentrates Feeds that provide a high level of nutrition in small amounts.

Conformation The way in which the horse is put together.

Corns Bruising of the sole between the wall of the hoof and the heel.

Courbette A movement in *haute ecole* where the horse stands almost upright on bent hind legs and leaps forward.

Cow pony A ranch horse used to work cattle.

Curb bit A mouthpiece with cheekpiece and chain used with a snaffle in a double bridle.

Curry comb (a) A metal comb that is used to clean the dirt from a body brush; (b) rubber ones can be used to removed dried-on dirt and mud.

Cutting horse A horse that has been

trained to separate selected cattle from a herd.

Dam The mother of a foal.

Dandy brush A stiff, long-bristled brush for removing dirt and mud from a horse's coat.

Dished face A concave head profile.

Dock The part of the tail where the hair grows and the hairless underside of the tail.

Double bridle A bridle made up of two bits—the bridoon and curb—normally used with two sets of reins.

Driving trials The competitive sport of carriage driving involving a three-phase test of dressage, marathon, and cones.

Egg-butt A type of snaffle.

Endurance riding A competitive sport where horses compete across long distances with compulsory veterinary checks along the way.

Entire A male horse that has not been castrated (i.e., gelded)

Ergots Horny growths on the back of the fetlock joint.

Eventing A three-phase competition comprising dressage, cross-country, and show jumping, held over one, two, or three days.

Ewe neck The neck is concave along its upper edge.

Faults Accrued in show jumping and cross-country when the horse knocks down, refuses, runs out, or falls at a fence.

FEI The Fédération Equestre Internationale—the governing body of international equestrian sport.

Fetlock The area at the back of the horse's leg, just above the hoof, where a tuft of hair grows.

Filly A female horse up to the age of four years.

Flat racing Racing over fixed distances without obstacles to jump.

Foal A young horse up to the age of 12 months.

Frog Rubbery pad at the base of the horse's foot that acts as a shock-absorber.

Fullering The groove in the base of a shoe that ensures a firmer foothold.

Gait Patterns of leg movement in the paces of the horse that include walk, trot, canter, and gallop. Specialized gaits practiced by some breeds include the paso, rack, and tolt.

Gallop A rapid four-beat pace.

Gaskin Or "second thigh," the area from above the hock toward the stifle.

Gauchos South American cowboys

Gelding A castrated male horse.

Girth (a) The circumference of the body measured from behind the withers; (b) the strap that is attached to the saddle and passed underneath the horse's belly to secure it. It is usually made from leather, nylon, or webbing.

Going Refers to the state of the ground, usually in racing, point-to-pointing, or cross-country.

Hackamore A bitless bridle

Half-bred A cross between a Thoroughbred and any other breed.

Hand A unit of measurement for horses. One hand is equivalent to 4 inches (10.16 cm).

Harriers Hounds used to hunt foxes and hares.

Haute ecole The classical method of equitation.

Haylege Preserved forage sold in sealed bags.

Hay Dried grass used as bulk feed.

Headcollar A bitless headpiece that is used for leading or tying up a horse.

Heavy horse Any draft breed such as Shire, Suffolk Punch, and Percheron.

Hemp An absorbent form of bedding made from the stem of the hemp plant.

Hobbles Light straps worn on pacers to connect the legs on the same side; they make breaking out of the gait more difficult.

Hock The backward-bending joints in the horse's hind legs.

Hogged mane The mane is removed by clipping.

Hoof pick A metal instrument used for removing mud, stones, etc. from the hoof.

Hoof wall The outer part of the hoof, which is divided into the toe, quarters (or sides), and heel.

Hot-shoeing The method of shoeing where the shoe is applied hot to achieve amore precise fit.

Hotting up A horse that becomes unduly excited.

Hurlingham Polo Association The governing body for polo in the United Kingdom.

In-foal Used to describe a pregnant mare.

In front of the bit When a horse is said to be pulling heavily on the hand.

In-hand classes Showing classes where the horse is led around, rather than ridden, and judged on conformation and condition.

Jockey Rides a horse in a race.

Join-up A method of starting a horse pioneered by the American Monty Roberts.

Kimblewick A type of bit.

Kür Freestyle dressage to music.

Laminitis Inflammation of the membranes (laminae) that lie between the wall of the hoof and the pedal bone.

Levade A movement in *haute ecole* in which the horse performs a controlled half-rear, with its forefeet drawn in and its hind legs deeply bent at the haunches.

Linseed The seed of flax that is fed in the form of jelly or tea.

Long-rein A method of schooling where the trainer follows the horse and controls it by means of long reins running either side of its body.

Low-, medium-, high-goal Different levels at which the game of polo is played.

Lungeing Controlling the horse on a circle from the ground.

Manege An enclosed space used for schooling horses.

Martingale An arrangement of straps designed to help keep the horse's head in the correct position.

Mare A female horse of four years or more.

Mouthing-bit A specially designed bit used when backing a horse.

Mud fever Inflammation of the horse's skin, generally caused by damp or muddy conditions.

National Hunt racing Where horses are raced over obstacles.

Navicular A bone in the heel of the horse.

Near-side The horse's left side

New Zealand rug A waterproof rug used on horses that are kept at grass.

Noseband The part of the bridle that goes across the horse's nose.

Numnah A padded cloth that is placed beneath the saddle.

Off-side The horse's right side.

On the bit When the horse is working with the correct head position and its mouth a little below the rider's hands.

Outcross The mating of unrelated horses.

Over-reach When the heel of the foreleg is struck by the toe of the hind leg.

Pacing A lateral gait used by horses in harness racing.

Pelham A bit that is designed to have the same effects as the two pieces of the double bridle but in one mouthpiece.

Point-to-pointing Amateur racing over fixed fences, organized by individual hunts.

Polocross A version of lacrosse played on horseback, using a long-handled net to carry and pass the ball.

Polo A mounted game using a stick and ball and played between teams of four.

Pommel The slightly raised front part of the saddle.

Pony Club A worldwide organization for young people up to the age of 21.

Private driving A form of showing where horses and carriages are judged on turnout and performance.

Puissance A show-jumping competition where the height of the final fence is increased until only one competitor remains.

Pulled (mane or tail) Hairs are removed from the underside of the mane and the sides of the tail to improve appearance.

Quartering A quick groom before exercising.

Racing plates Lightweight shoes worn by racehorses.

Rack A fast, four-beat gait employed by the American Saddlebred horse.

Rasp A tool used in shoeing to smooth rough edges.

Road and tracks Part of the speed and endurance phase of a three-day event.

Rodeo The American Wild West event

Roller A broad strap that goes around the horse's body and is used to hold a rug in place.

Roman nose A convex head profile.

Saddle-bronc One of the classic or standard events of a rodeo that requires the rider to remain on a bucking horse with only a modified stock saddle and rope for reins.

Saddle A seat for the rider on horseback. Specific designs are used for different disciplines, such as show-jumping, showing, sidesaddle, dressage, racing, and Western riding.

Sarcoids Tumors of the skin

Schoolmaster An older, experienced horse.

Seat Position of the rider on the horse.

Shavings An alternative type of bedding made from wood.

Shire packs The term used to describe the famous hunts located around the Midlands region of England.

Shoes Usually made of steel and worn to protect the horse's feet from wear and tear.

Sire The father of a foal.

Snaffle The simplest type of bit, which consists of a single bar with a ring at each end from which the reins are attached. A number of variations are available.

Sole The thin protective layer on the underneath of the foot.

Stable rubber Cloth used at the end of grooming to give a final polish.

Steeplechase A course of a specified distance involving a number of fixed obstacles to jump.

Steer wrestling A rodeo event where the cowboy chases a steer and, when in position, throws himself from his horse and wrestles the animal onto its side.

Stifle The joint above the hock in a horse's hind leg.

Stirrup irons Suspended from the saddle by leathers to support the rider's foot and made from metal, wood, or leather.

Stock saddle A Western saddle with high pommel and cantle and long flaps.

Strangles A disease of the upper respiratory tract, often occurring in young horses.

Studs (a) A place where horses are kept for breeding purposes; (b) a metal head screwed into specially made holes in the shoe to give a firmer grip.

Succulents Foods such as carrots and apples.

Sugar beet The remains of the root vegetable after the sugar has been taken out. It comes in either pulp or cube form and must be soaked before use.

Sulky A lightweight cart used in harness racing.

Sweet itch Severe dermatitis mainly affecting the mane, poll, and root of the tail, but in severe cases also the neck, shoulders, and hindquarters.

Tetanus A serious disease caused by a micro-organism that lives in soil and enters the horse's body through wounds.

Tetrathlon A sport involving running, riding, shooting, and swimming.

Thoroughbred A purebred horse; Arabian and Turkish stallions crossed with English mares largely for racing purposes.

Throatlash Part of the bridle that fastens underneath the horse's throat.

Thrush Inflammation of the frog of the horse's foot.

Timber racing Amateur sport of racing over fixed timber obstacles.

Tree The foundation part of the saddle, normally constructed from laminated wood, plastic, or fiberglass.

Trot A two-time pace where the horse's legs move in diagonal pairs.

Tail male line Descent through the male parent line.

Tolt The fast, running walk pace of the Icelandic Horse.

Warmbloods Generally used to describe a half- or part-bred horse that is the result of Thoroughbred or Arab crosses with other blood or bloods.

Weight classes Hunters and cobs are shown in weight divisions—light-, medium-, and heavyweight.

Walk A four-time pace.

Well-sprung ribs Long, rounded ribs that allow plenty of space for lung expansion.

Withers The area at the base of the neck, between the shoulderblades. The place from which a horse's height is measured.

Whipper-in Assistant to the huntsman of a pack of hounds.

Wisp Made of twisted hay or straw and used to harden muscles and increase circulation.

Xenophen Greek soldier and historian who provided the basis for classical equitation.

index